The Facilitative Leader

The Facilitative Leader

Behaviors That Enable Success

R. Glenn Ray

Prentice Hall
Upper Saddle River, NJ 07458

Library of Congress Cataloging-in-Publication Data

Ray, R. Glenn.
    The facilitative leader : behaviors that enable success / R. Glenn
Ray.
    p. cm.
    Includes bibliographical references and index.
    ISBN 0-13-895228-0
    1. Group facilitation. 2. Leadership I. Title
HD66.R3918 1999
658.4'092—dc21   98-40499
                                                   CIP

Acquisitions Editor: Elizabeth Sugg
Director of Production and Manufacturing: Bruce Johnson
Managing Editor: Mary Carnis
Editorial/Production Supervision and Interior Design:
    Inkwell Publishing Services
Cover Design: Miguel Ortiz
Manufacturing Buyer: Edward O' Dougherty

Printed in the United States of America

Reprinted with corrections June, 1999

10 9 8 7 6 5 4 3 2

ISBN 0-13-895228-0

Prentice-Hall International (UK) Limited, *London*
Prentice-Hall of Australia Pty. Limited, *Sydney*
Prentice-Hall Canada Inc., *Toronto*
Prentice-Hall Hispanoamericana, S.A., *Mexico*
Prentice-Hall of India Private Limited, *New Delhi*
Prentice-Hall of Japan, Inc., *Tokyo*
Prentice-Hall of Southeast Asia Pte. Ltd., *Singapore*
Editora Prentice-Hall do Brasil, Ltda., *Rio de Janeiro*

Contents

2 Enabler of Change   25

3 Respectful Communicator   45

Contents vii

7
Manager of Conflict   *131*

8
Small Group Facilitator   *149*

9
Conclusion   *159*

References   *165*

Index   *169*

Preface

Leadership is an increasingly important topic for discussion in all organizations and society as a whole. It is one thing to understand the theories and constructs of leadership, as well as that understanding is necessary, but it is more important to be able to demonstrate the behaviors of successful leaders and enable others to develop these skills. The purpose of this book is to illustrate these leader behaviors and to provide an opportunity for the reader to practice them.

The word *enable* is prominently featured throughout the book. This word represents a key concept important to all leaders. Leaders are not successful by themselves. Success is the result of effort expended by all organizational members. In this country we have accomplished a great transformation in the structure of business organizations in the last decade. These changes have improved the competitive advantage of American business. Unfortunately, this success has resulted in a great decline in employee loyalty. Many organizational members feel less secure and less valued than they did ten years ago. This decline is dangerous and threatens our future success. Many organizations have in their mission or vision statements something to the effect that people come first. This book suggest ways of making that belief a reality through more respectful communication.

Prominently featured in this work are the illustrative and sometimes humorous stories sprinkled throughout the chapters. Over the years I have had a good response to the many seminars and presentations I have made on organizational communication topics. In writing this book, I tried to capture the best of the training programs, especially the stories and illustrations of events that have happened to me or that have been related to me. My intent was to capture the tone of an actual training program.

Audience

The Facilitative Leader: Behaviors that Enable Success was written for a variety of audiences. It was designed as a text for academic classes in leadership, communication, and management. In addition, the book is appropriate for leaders and followers at all levels of organizations. The book best serves these readers if they focus on creating personal development plans with specific behavioral goals. Other audiences include organizational trainers and human resource managers. The contents of the book could be used as a model for organization development through improved employee leadership behaviors.

Overview of Contents

Chapter 1 introduces the definition of leadership that is used throughout the book. Several key leadership theories and studies that span the last hundred years are described, linked, and tracked. The variety of leadership behaviors demonstrated by successful leaders is detailed, including relationship building, coaching, problem solving, and action planning. Other elements of leadership, such as use of humor and coping with change and chaos, are discussed. Finally, the five modes of the facilitative leader are outlined.

Chapter 2 defines the role of the facilitative leader as a change agent. The concept of enabling is described and prescribed for the reader. Change is by definition a critical part of leadership. In this chapter, change is described as an everyday choice that we all frequently make in our daily lives. People react differently to change. Demographics of change common in organizations are described. They include the Change Champion, Fence Sitters, and the "Hell! No!

We Won't Go" groups. The relationship between risk taking and learning is explored. Finally, visioning and a change model are explained.

The third chapter is dedicated to a foundation of effective leadership behaviors: respectful communication. Respect is the key word in this chapter. We all communicate differently. This chapter describes how our field of experience defines why we communicate the way we do. Ways of connecting between two people to create shared understanding are explored. The importance of nonverbal communication to shared understanding is expressed in detail. Finally, a specific set of nonverbal and verbal behaviors is described as listening.

Chapter 4 focuses on a means of helping employees improve their skills so that they can more effectively meet the organization's needs. The value of promoting learning among organizational members is detailed. Learning techniques are described. The field of study called adult learning is reviewed. Several processes for employee development are offered.

The fifth chapter describes a comprehensive model for creating effective teams. Proven modules for team development are explained in detail. This chapter allows organizational trainers to design a custom training program. Techniques for setting the foundation for team communication are set forth. How groups are most effectively developed is explained using a descriptive model. The process of dealing with conflict using a structure adapted from Fisher and Ury's *Getting to Yes* is utilized. The importance of problem-solving and goal-setting skills are emphasized. Finally, a process for engineering greater shared communication among all team members is delivered.

A series of problem-solving tools is elaborated in Chapter 6. First a simple model is explained. Then, a variety of techniques are offered for defining the problem, prioritizing issues, analyzing the problem, making the decision, and implementing the solution. The entire process is illustrated with a comprehensive illustration of a real life problem. Finally, more effective ways of efficiently running team problem-solving meetings are described.

Chapter 7 deals with conflict in organizations. Conflict resolution is replaced by the phrase *conflict management.* Conflict will always be with us, and we should not ignore its positive outcomes. It is not desirable to eliminate conflict. Rather, we need to use it as a tool to create positive products. Common feelings about conflict are explored. The negative impact of the concept of Groupthink on team creativity is explained. The use of the Thomas-Kilmann Conflict Styles

Inventory is illustrated. The role of feedback in mediating conflict is described. A feedback scripting process called E-FAB is detailed.

Chapter 8 helps us understand the behaviors of a competent facilitator and how these skills aid leaders and organizations. Specific behaviors of facilitators are described. Specific techniques for involving participants and dealing with resistance are described. Finally, integrating the concept of facilitation into the daily behaviors of organizational members who are filling the roles of leaders, followers, and neutral discussion leaders is explored.

This book is, as are all books, a labor of love. My life has been focused on learning how to improve my leadership skills. In this work, I have tried to capture these learnings. My hope is that it will help you as it has helped thousands of internal and external clients over the last fifteen years of daily practice.

Acknowledgments

This book has resulted from over twenty-five years of thinking about and practicing leadership skills that I have learned from family, supervisors, peers, professors, and associates. There are too many to mention them all here. However, I would like to attempt to identify some of the most influential ones.

The most important figures who modeled leadership for me were my parents, Will B. and Audrey Ray. My dad always encouraged me to place myself in leadership roles, which I did in spite of an intense fear of being in front of groups. Mom showed me a persistence to do the right things and unconditional love.

Other significant influences on my development of this model include Dr. Sue DeWine who is one of the best facilitative leaders I have known. She agreed to take on an ex-coal miner as a graduate student and research assistant. I watched her and attempted to imitate her skill set. She taught me and helped me develop as a facilitator and communication consultant. I appreciate the time she spent reviewing this book.

Tim Fidler showed me how that skill set could be used in the workplace. He was respectful and humorous. I valued his abilities and added what I learned from him to my repertoire.

In the specific writing of this book, I must thank Dr. Stephen Schwartz. He gave of his personal time to review and improve this manuscript. With great detail, he critiqued two versions of the manuscript. As my supervisor and personal hero, he also supported me and gave me freedom as I invented a training and development company. I place him as the best boss that I have ever had.

Cathy Brown was a tremendous supporter in the writing of this book. When I had doubts, she encouraged me. She also gave many grammatical and stylistic suggestions that improved this work. Myra Reich made my life easier during the production of this work. She was one of the more effective office managers that I have ever seen. She organized my documents and kept me straight throughout this process. She also gave me many valuable suggestions for modifying this work. Sid Potash reviewed Chapter 1, for which I am grateful. Donna Graham painstakingly proofread the first printing which I greatly appreciate.

There are so many others who reviewed all or parts of this work and from whom I learned. My brothers Jack and Joe, my sister Sylvia Tatum, and my mother all made valuable comments on early drafts. Jeff Barnes made a number of valued suggestions on the entire book. He is a friend and role model. Dave Richardson, Roger Thorne, Shirley Williams-Kirksey, Bob Hall, and Sandra Kolankiewicz gave me support and encouragement throughout this process.

My children Betsy and Elijah were patient as I tested my stories and theories on them repeatedly. Their love and encouragement was especially important to me.

In addition, I would like to thank my niece, Audrey Tatum, Bernie Muiznieks, Myra Reich, Jen Halstead, and Janice Thomas for illustrations that they created during training sessions or specifically for this book. Stephen Carr also allowed me to include portions of his company's cultural descriptors, which I greatly appreciate.

Others who read and contributed ideas on this book include Laurie Kiefe, Kathy Ownby, as well as a number of undergraduate and graduate students in classes that I taught. Finally, Roberta Chamberlin and Leah Anderson helped me in the revisions of the final draft. I am grateful to all of the above who helped me in this significant endeavor. Thank you.

R. GLENN RAY

About the Author

Glenn Ray has had twenty-seven years as an organizational member and fifteen years of experience as an internal and external consultant conducting over 1000 workshops on organization development topics, such as leadership, team development, facilitator training, interpersonal communication, managing conflict, change management, and problem solving and decision making techniques. His training focuses on building relationships with his clients in order to enhance behavioral change. He also consults with companies regarding organization development processes and performance issues.

Glenn spent two years in the construction industry, nine years in the mining industry, four years in the chemical industry as an internal consultant, one year in manufacturing, and the last nine years as an external consultant working for the McDonough Center for Leadership and Business at Marietta College in Marietta, Ohio. His organizational roles include carpenter helper, union worker in the United Mine Workers of America (UMWA), supervisor of production workers, mid-level manager of training in a plant of 1,000 employees, and corporate training director.

Additionally, Glenn teaches leadership and communication courses at Marietta College. He has published eight articles in national journals, four chapters in books, and numerous conference presentations.

Glenn earned a bachelor's degree in psychology, a master's degree in guidance and counseling and student personnel services, and a doctorate in interpersonal communication, all from Ohio University.

For fun, Glenn has rafted the Colorado River through the Grand Canyon, traveled to see a solar eclipse in Hawaii, hiked volcanoes in Costa Rica, attended after-carnival festivities in Tobago, and explored Mayan temples in Belize and Guatemala. He has visited all fifty states and rafted, canoed, or kayaked in 13 states and four countries.

Glenn can be reached at Marietta College by phone at 1-800-767-4622 or by e-mail at rayg@marietta.edu.

The Facilitative Leader

What Is Leadership?

Leadership Definition

Leadership is a series of behaviors that enable a group or organization to accomplish commonly desired goals. You cannot lead a group to the place where they presently are. You can possibly manage or maintain a status quo. However, in today's chaotic environment, the desire and ability to maintain the status quo have eroded. One of the purposes of leadership is to enable all organizational members to choose to move in a common direction and to accomplish their organizational tasks successfully while learning from the tasks and growing as people. Bass (1990) suggests that, "Leadership is an interaction between two or more members of a group that often involves a structuring or restructuring of the situation and the perceptions and expectations of the members" (p. 19). As people come together in an organization to accomplish goals they hold in common, communication skills are keys to the success a leader will have with these interpersonal interactions.

Leadership does not occur only at the top of an organization. If an organization is to survive the rapid changes of today's and tomorrow's work environment, effective leadership must be demonstrated at each

1

of the organization's levels. An illustration of leadership at a surprising organizational level occurred while I was a coal miner in the UMWA (United Mine Workers of America). At the time, the early 1970s, wildcat strikes were common. On one particular day, the shift foreman stood at the elevator signifying the beginning of the shift. I started to move toward the elevator but noticed that no one else was following me. I looked around and saw everyone standing against the walls, glaring at me. I stepped to the side in alignment with the rest of the men. For over half an hour we all stood there with the shift foreman pleading with us to go to work. Finally, Wally stepped away from the wall and onto the elevator. One by one the rest of us followed. Not a word was said. Wally was an informal leader of the group. The leadership we witnessed that day was entirely nonverbal and proved that leadership is demonstrated at all levels, not just in the management ranks and not always for the organization's good. Leadership can either support or oppose organizational objectives.

Evolution of Leadership Studies

Leadership has been discussed and studied for years. Throughout most of our history, leaders were described by the Great Man theory. Leaders were seen as men of stature and inborn talent, hence the reliance on monarchies. By the beginning of the twentieth century, researchers were beginning to identify traits of leaders. Unfortunately, the problem with trait research is that each of the various studies identified different traits (VanFleet and Yukl, 1989). Thus, there was little agreement on a common set of leadership qualities.

Around the turn of the century, Fredrick Taylor, an industrial engineer, was designing the scientific management system. Scientific management was based upon the assumption that if you could isolate productivity variables, you could improve an organization's performance by increasing the efficiencies of the individual variables. Although Taylor intended to improve the working conditions and salaries of the average worker (Weisbord, 1987), his system is most remembered for segmenting work into artificially small components for efficiency's sake. Many of today's progressive organizational change processes are intended to reverse Taylor's segmentation of work. The purpose of this reversal is to create more worker ownership for the customer's end product. It will take facilitative leaders at all levels of an organization to capitalize on today's new management requirements.

In 1924, a famous series of studies that pioneered a new approach to leading organizations, the Human Relations Approach, also called the Hawthorne Studies, was initiated (Mayo, 1947). The Hawthorne studies (Roethlisberger, 1939) were administered at a Western Electric Company plant in Illinois, Hawthorne being the name of the plant where the studies were conducted. Designed to build upon the scientific management theories, one of the studies focused on lighting in the plant and its effects on the workers. Of course, the hypothesis was that increased lighting at some optimal level would result in increased job performance. The first few stages of the research did seem to support the hypothesis. Just to check the validity of the research results, the researchers reduced the lighting levels in the area being studied. To their amazement, they found that productivity continued to increase even after the lighting was reduced. The improvements continued until the lighting was so poor that the workers couldn't accomplish their work. This outcome confounded the Harvard researchers. After extended deliberation, the researchers proposed that the findings resulted from the attention the workers received from the researchers. The workers took more pride in their work and their performance improved as a result of the researchers' attention. Consequently, the focus was redirected to employees as the primary source of productivity improvement.

Beginning in the late 1930s, a series of organizational leadership theories that built upon the Hawthorne studies was being developed at the universities of Iowa, Ohio State, and Michigan. The Iowa studies defined leaders as democratic, autocratic, or laissez-faire. Group performance and attitudes were the focus of this study. Laissez-faire leaders who basically did nothing were judged worst on both variables. Autocratic leaders had the best performance, and democratic leaders had the best attitudes. The problem with the autocratic leaders was that when they left the room, work ceased and horseplay and bickering began. When democratic or laissez-faire leaders left the room, work continued, and decision making went forward. Democratic leaders were found to be the most effective (Lewin, Lippitt, and White, 1939). The Ohio State studies described leadership as a matrix of two orientations. These theories categorized leaders as task (structuring) or relationship (consideration) oriented (Stogdill and Shartle, 1948). Task oriented leaders communicate primarily on getting the job done. Relationship oriented leaders are concerned with people and maintaining positive relationships. The prescription of the research was for a combined high task and relationship style. Later,

Hersey and Blanchard's (1982) research modified the Ohio State findings by suggesting that the appropriate leadership style depended upon the followers' willingness and ability to do the job. New employees needed more task oriented leadership. As employees gained more experience, the leader should move toward a more relationship oriented interaction. As skills became solidified, the leader should delegate more and be available based upon the follower's needs. The Michigan studies found that effective supervisors focused on subordinates (employee-centered) rather than just on getting the task accomplished (job-centered) (Likert, 1967). Likert also developed the "linking pin" theory, which stated that all leaders are also followers in another context. He described a System 4 participatory type of organization and recommended that leaders attempt to emulate it. System 1 organizations are described as traditional and autocratic. System 4 organizations employ leadership that involves and supports employees in goal setting and decision making. Employees have more control in the System 4 organization (Weihrich and Rigny, 1980). Likert designed a questionnaire that measured the level of participation an organization demonstrates and identified actions that move the organization to be more participative.

Douglas McGregor (1960) called the task-focused leader a Theory X leader and the relationship-focused leader a Theory Y leader. He also proposed that the more successful leader was the Theory Y leader. Theory Y leaders believe that most workers come to work wanting to do a good job, will work to their skill level, and want to make a contribution. Theory X leaders, on the other hand, believe that workers are lazy and have to be driven if work is to be accomplished. These theories are demonstrated every day by behaviors of leaders and by orientation processes of new leaders. When I became a supervisor, the training I received was not formal. It occurred following the Friday afternoon shift where my boss, my peers, and I were bellied up to a local bar in Malaga, Ohio. I heard messages such as, "You gotta watch 'em like a hawk," "They (union men) will work harder getting out of work than working," and "If you turn your back, they'll stab you." I remember thinking, I was one of them only a few weeks ago. I didn't think I was that bad. The assumptions we support, whether Theory X or Theory Y, impact our leadership styles and our interactions with all organizational members.

The facilitative leader favors the Theory Y leadership style but with a strong concern for task accomplishment. Leadership is a series of communication behaviors. The leader truly gets work done through

---

Leadership Theory Comparison Chart

Leadership Studies	Relationship	Task
Iowa Study	Democratic	Autocratic
Ohio State Study	Consideration	Initiating Structure
Michigan Study	Employee Centered	Job Centered
MacGregor	Theory Y	Theory X

---

communicating with others. Also, it is important to note that productive relationships are defined and improved, or damaged, by the communication of both parties.

Modern Approaches: Fads or Learning Process

As practitioners have attempted to operationalize the evolution of leadership theory, some have judged the results fads. But I view the changes in terms of learning and skill building. That is, processes such as participative management, quality of work life, quality circles, employee involvement, Self-Directed Work Teams (SDWT), and Total Quality Management (TQM) have resulted from prior learning and have been implemented in order to improve organizational performance.

My first experience with organizational change leadership was as a supervisor in the underground coal industry in the late 1970s (Ray, 1993; Ray and Ray, 1995). The company I worked for had suddenly lost its long-term contracts with a power company in Cleveland. The price of coal per ton per worker had to be slashed in order to compete on the open market. The company's leaders instituted a process called participative management, developed by Trist in England shortly after World War II (Weisbord, 1987). Participative management involves a less directive style which seeks more decision making and input by workers. The supervisors were taught this process by the mine foreman, who is the site operations manager, in five 8-hour sessions on consecutive Saturdays. The mine foreman had previously attended a

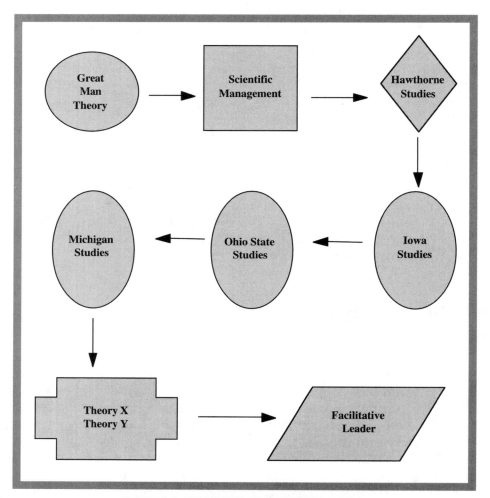

FIGURE 1-1. EVOLUTION OF LEADERSHIP THEORY

series of training programs with other organizational leaders and learned the process. Months later, partly as a result of the new behavior patterns of supervisors and managers and partly as a result of job security fears, productivity doubled.

I learned from this process that, as a supervisor, I didn't have to take total ownership of all of the day's work. I wouldn't lose power or control by encouraging and allowing others to make decisions. In fact, everyone felt better about the day's productivity. This new way of doing work made sense to me, but I had to overturn the traditional supervisor's paradigm. Barker (1992) describes this paradigm switch from the traditional expectation that "[S]upervisors' roles are to think and keep people busy; workers' roles are to keep busy and not to think" to the new paradigm of "[B]rains are best on the line; supervisors must tap all that intelligence so that together the workers and the supervisors can solve the problems" (p. 132).

Later I moved to a chemical company as the training manager of its largest manufacturing site. My mandate from the plant manager was to implement "employee involvement" among plant employees. I began by reviewing research on quality of work life and quality circles. Literature describing quality of work life processes reminded me that a person's surroundings impact job satisfaction and thereby commitment to the task. Job satisfaction has an impact on productivity, but its primary contribution to work levels is to set the stage for true employee commitment. I also found a positive correlation between the level of satisfaction of employees with the amount and type of communication in which they are involved and their perception of the amount of influence they have at work (Ray, 1988).

Early on, the research into quality circles indicated that the result was tremendous growth in employee commitment to the organization. However, the process also encouraged employees to think in a "pay for ideas only" mentality: "I'll give you this improvement idea if you pay me a percentage of the economic benefit." This mentality can cut employees off from feelings of larger ownership in the organization. But we learned from quality circles that employees can be excited at work if we tap their knowledge and experience. It is also evident that companies can improve profits by soliciting and implementing employee ideas.

Employee involvement leveraged the key learnings from quality circles and focused on transferring skills to all employees (Ray, Hines, & Wilcox, 1994; Ray & Stapleton, 1998). Team members were taught communication skills, problem-solving and decision-making skills, and how to interpret organizational financial data for decision making. Work floor operators were given organizational information that previously had been held at the vice president's level. We learned that decision making is most effectively and appropriately done by the people who perform the work, a view supported by Max Depree (1992), who suggests that organizational power does not guarantee wisdom.

SDWT Model Description

Self-Directed Work Teams (SDWT) became popular in the 1990s. To my mind, this system of work is a natural progression of employee involvement. Employee involvement enables employees to give input on a variety of problems. SDWT members are taught the administrative and communication skills of their former supervisors, and then team members' jobs are enlarged. Decision making is delegated to the team and supported by new organizational policies and systems (Ray, 1995). Leadership training is also needed to enable the traditional supervisor to make the transition to team coach. Team training to meet the development needs of the team members is critical to the success of the SDWT.

To create SDWTs, organizational members should first research other organizations that are attempting to make a similar change. Literature reviews will identify these organizations. Contact can be made and site visits arranged to share information about organizational efforts and their successes and problems. From these visits benchmarks can be created from best practices that can be emulated.

Second, analyze the technical skills of the organization's workforce. In the past, the supervisor was often the technical expert. This skill set must be transferred to the workers. Usually, this is a tremendous task because of the time and resources needed to develop the training materials and train the workforce. The results, however, will impact the bottom line even if you aren't moving to SDWTs.

Third, have sessions with all employees to explain and discuss the reasons for making the change and the process that will be undertaken.

Fourth, dedicate people to lead this process. They should be given small group facilitator training that incorporates problem-solving techniques.

Fifth, assess each group's team development needs and design a custom program to meet those needs. Common topics often include communication, interpersonal relationships, conflict management, and problem-solving techniques.

Sixth, give coaching, feedback, and timely business information to the team as they meet to communicate and solve problems.

TQM Model Description

In the late 1980s TQM (Total Quality Management) appeared in the literature. Born from the work of Edward Deming, Joseph Juran, and others, it placed another block on the structure of the organizational change

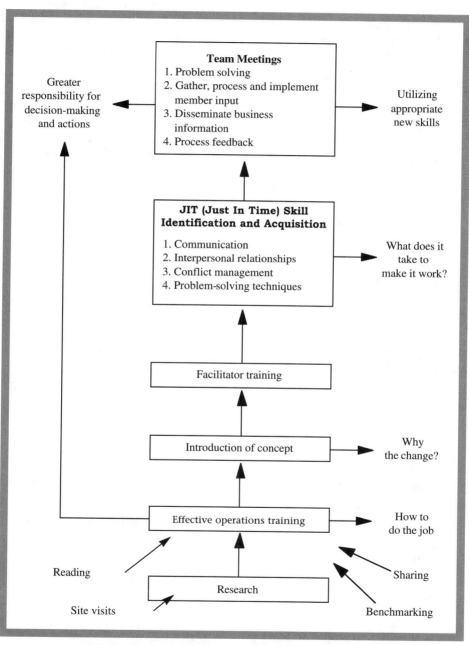

FIGURE 1-2. SELF-DIRECTED WORK TEAM TRAINING MODEL

process. The process utilizes the learning of both participative management and employee involvement: that decision making is more effective if it is done by those doing the work. The concepts developed under the "quality of work life" banner are implemented in the TQM process when all employees respect the ideas and needs of individuals regardless of their organizational status. The ideas developed by quality circles are leveraged as cross-functional organizational members are brought together to solve problems, although from a system perspective. Principles of employee involvement are implemented by transferring skills and information in ways that shatter the organizational paradigms. Together, these ideas result in incremental continuous performance improvement. One successful TQM organization development model is described in Figure 1-3 (Ray and Brown, 1997).

This model shows the consultant's proposed development model and the final process that was implemented by the client.

First, a training program was designed to introduce the concept of TQM (Total Quality Management).

Second, interviews were conducted by the consultant to determine specific needs that the process could address.

Third, the management staff designed a vision statement to guide the process.

Fourth, a facilitator training program was administered to develop internal consultants who would lead the continuous process improvement teams.

Fifth, a two-day training program on quality problem-solving tools was designed and administered. After the consultant taught two of these programs with the internal facilitators, he handed the program to the internal facilitators who taught the rest of the organizational members.

Sixth, brainstorming sessions were held with all employees to define the most important areas to focus cross-functional process improvement teams.

Seventh, a steering committee representing all constituencies of the organization was formed to assist cross-functional teams in implementing their process improvement solutions.

Eighth, expectations communication sessions were held with all intact work groups to clarify needs and work responsibilities.

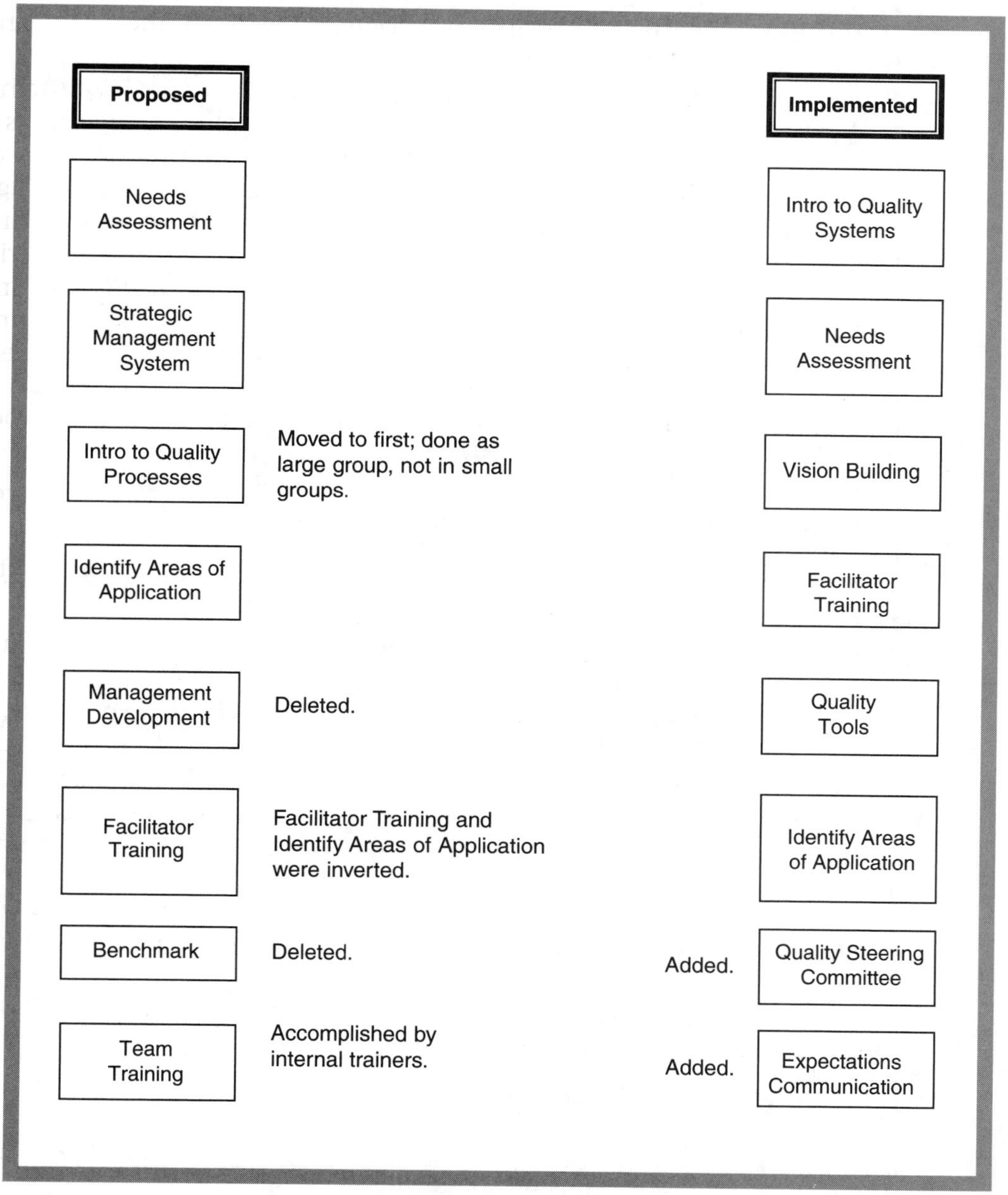

Proposed		Implemented
Needs Assessment		Intro to Quality Systems
Strategic Management System		Needs Assessment
Intro to Quality Processes	Moved to first; done as large group, not in small groups.	Vision Building
Identify Areas of Application		Facilitator Training
Management Development	Deleted.	Quality Tools
Facilitator Training	Facilitator Training and Identify Areas of Application were inverted.	Identify Areas of Application
Benchmark	Deleted.	Added. Quality Steering Committee
Team Training	Accomplished by internal trainers.	Added. Expectations Communication

FIGURE 1-3. TQM FLOWCHART
TQM INTERVENTION AT MR/DD
(WASHINGTON COUNTY BOARD OF MENTALLY RETARDED AND DEVELOPMENTALLY DISABLED)

The reengineering concept developed by Hammer and Champy (1993) employs TQM concepts but focuses on fundamentally reinventing an organizational process while employing present technology. In the reengineering procedure, the present process is set on the shelf, and the customer needs are examined at the same time that two critical questions are asked: "What is the simplest way or what are the fewest steps required to meet the customer's needs?" and "How can we use technology in an optimal way to meet the customer's needs?"

One bank president I know would like to offer a new home loan in thirty minutes. A way to move toward that goal is to map all of the steps to approve a loan and then time the actual work required to accomplish each step. Then the waiting time between steps can be eliminated and new ways of doing the steps faster can be invented. Transferring the loan file from step to step on e-mail might be one way of speeding up the process and using technology more effectively. Another option is to cross-train employees to be able to perform several steps rather than transferring the file so frequently.

In today's competitive environment, continuous performance improvement is a critical necessity. Organizations don't need consultants whose focus is to "fix" an organization or its culture. I don't even believe that is possible. We need learning organizations whose members are experimenting with new processes and adding problem-solving and processing skills to their repertoires (Senge, 1990). External resources need to be focused on "handing the ball off" to internal resources. The energies and intelligence of America's workers are more than enough to ensure competitive success if they are developed and focused effectively.

The word facilitator comes from the Latin root, Facilis, which means "to make easy." In this book I describe the key set of behaviors exhibited by the effective facilitative leader of the future: relationship building, coaching, learning, problem solving, action planning, and implementation tracking.

Relationship Building

The facilitative leader understands group dynamics and makes communication within a group more effective by developing shared understanding. The facilitative leader has a unique communication style that effectively opens the communication atmosphere in a group. All work is accomplished through relationships. Facilitation is a respectful way of interacting among peers and among those in reporting relationships. When leaders use facilitative behaviors, relationships are improved and increased willingness to work together is realized. Another aspect of relationship building is giving the employee time to express personal concerns and opinions. I call this *face time*. Face time should occur on a regular basis.

Coaching

The facilitative leader acts as both a coach and a learner. The facilitative leader is willing to teach other employees anything the other employees want or need to know. The days of holding information close to the chest as a power source are gone.

Learning

Think about those in your life who taught you something that you still value and use. How do you feel about these people? You would probably be glad to help them should they need your help. More effective and long-term power sources result from teaching and learning from one another.

Problem Solving

Facilitative leaders approach work life in a problem-solving mode. Blaming is irrelevant and a tremendous waste of time. The facilitative leader focuses on improving processes and finding fixes, not on punishing mistakes. Mistakes are learning processes and should be discussed, not hidden. Many problem-solving techniques are useful for organizing problem analysis. Problem solving is useful but means little if it does not result in action planning.

Action Planning and Implementation Tracking

The facilitative leader carries the improvement project forward by identifying what steps will be accomplished, when they will be accomplished, and who is responsible for each component. Finally, the plan is diagrammed and displayed prominently so that the implementation can be tracked.

Facilitative Leader Behaviors

When I discuss leadership with various organizational members, I often ask them to think of the best leader they have personally known. They describe a variety of effective behaviors:

♦ Communicates a clear and articulate vision.

♦ Gives me the feedback I need.

♦ Helps me realize when I haven't met expectations.

♦ Tells me when I do a good job.

♦ Identifies opportunities.

♦ Cares about me and my career.

♦ Listens well.

♦ Speaks in my language.

♦ Makes me feel like a valued, equal team member.

♦ Enables me to find solutions to my problems.

♦ Teaches me problem-solving techniques.

♦ Helps me think through conflicts.

♦ Enjoys using and interacting with humor.

One of the most common criticisms of leaders by their subordinates is the lack of clear vision. Effective leaders point the way to desired future behaviors and talk repeatedly to all employees about the vision, as described in Chapter 2. This direction helps employees to make the right choices daily in the many decisions for which they are responsible.

Identifying opportunities for subordinates is an important leadership skill. These opportunities may be to take on new job assignments or to be considered for promotions within the organization. Many leaders are afraid that if they identify opportunities, their staff will leave the company or department. Of course, this is a possibility. However, employee loyalty and commitment are escalated when the leader demonstrates deep concern for the employee's future. If an employee does leave, the leader's support will encourage the highest qualified employees of the organization to take the place of the employee who leaves.

Listening skills are probably the most important set of behaviors of an effective leader listed by employees. Listening takes time, but it pays revenues in positive relationship building. Listening is described in depth in Chapter 3 as a set of behaviors of the respectful communicator.

The respectful communicator attempts to speak in the language of employees. Technical jargon is not appropriate for all conversations. People who use jargon indiscriminately are seen as less respectful than those who try to remain aware of the understanding of the other person. If you want to communicate with me, speak in my language, not over my head.

Many of the facilitative behaviors mentioned so far help employees feel valued as equal team members. A more in-depth discussion about team development can be found in Chapter 4.

The facilitative leader not only talks employees through problems and uses the opportunity as a learning experience, but also teaches problem-solving techniques to employees. This concept is described in Chapter 5.

Feedback is critical to enable employees to continue positive behaviors and to change undesired behaviors. The process described in Chapter 6 is a useful template for constructing feedback. Feedback is the mechanism for helping employees understand when they are not meeting expectations and when they are doing a good job.

Use of Humor

Finally, facilitative leaders don't take themselves too seriously. They look at life with a sense of humor. I learned a lesson about leadership and humor while I was a supervisor in the coal mine. One day as I was proceeding to ferry a group of miners out of the mine at the end of the shift, I was seized by four miners, one at each of my arms and legs. Of course, I was surprised. They picked me up and laid me down on a flatcar. Next, they unbuttoned my bib overalls and began brushing my chest and face with a paint mixture made of red chalk dust and water. I admonished them repeatedly, but to no avail. My ego was trampled. When they finished, I got up, dressed, and climbed onto my jeep. I was steaming all the way out of the mine. In reality, I was not hurt, other than my ego.

After I reached the surface, I angrily stomped into the foremen's office covered with red paint. The mine superintendent burst into laughter when he saw me. Once he learned the whole story, the incident escalated beyond my control. Later, I had calmed down, but my crew members each received a reprimand letter in their files written by the mine superintendent. For the next several months, my crew committed themselves to personal battle against me to pay me back. Many a day after that, I wished I had not let my ego consume me and had instead taken a shower before entering the foremen's office. That event ushered in the worst year of my work life. Weeks later I learned that my boss, the shift foreman, had paid my crew half an hour overtime pay to paint me, so the letters in their files were pulled. However, the grudges against me were not as easily removed. Facilitative leaders don't take themselves too seriously. They know when to take a joke and when to take issue.

Humor is an important attribute of the facilitative leader. The timing can sometimes be difficult. I often tell a humorous story to illustrate the difficulty of leadership that was told to me by a peer when I was working with an archaeological survey crew in the Mark Twain National Forest in Missouri. It seems that a young man was driving through the Ozarks one day and noticed a strange sight in a nearby field: a pig with a peg leg. This sight amazed the young man, and he stopped his car and stared for a few moments. Finally, his curiosity roused, he proceeded down the road to the closest farmhouse. He parked the car, walked up to the front door, and knocked. A farmer with a long beard and wearing overalls came to the door. The young man apologized for bothering the farmer. He explained, "I was just driving by your farm and noticed that you had a pig with a peg leg. Could you tell me about that pig?" At the mention of the pig, the farmer beamed with pride. He said, "Let me tell you about that pig. That pig is the most wonderful leader pig in the world. A month ago I was out yonder plowing the field, and I hit a groundhog hole. The hole caved in and the tractor tipped over and trapped me. You know what that pig did? She bust out of the pen, led all the other pigs out to the tractor, and they rooted me out from under the tractor. Most wonderful leader pig in the world! Two weeks ago, the house caught on fire in the middle of the night. You know what that pig did? She bust out the pen again and broke down the door and woke me up, saved my life. Most wonderful leader pig in the world!" At this point the young man interrupted, "I can see that she is a mighty fine animal, but that doesn't explain her peg leg." The farmer wrinkled his face up in puzzlement, looked at the young man, and replied, "A wonderful leader pig like that, you can't eat it all at once."

DRAWING BY MYRA REICH

The moral of the story is that even an effective leader can be eaten alive. We all look at leadership differently. Given the personalities involved and unforeseen circumstances, even effective leadership can fail. There is no tried and true set of behaviors guaranteed to work with all people and in all situations. Humor can be an effective way to get important points across to others if you can make a linkage between the point being made and the punch line of the humor.

One organization I worked for had a very sober environment. No one ever seemed to be enjoying work. One Friday afternoon at about four o'clock, I decided to lighten up the place. I went to a couple of the secretaries and told the pig story. Each of them burst out in laughter. At just about that time, my boss, the president of the company, poked his head out of his office to see what the racket was. He beckoned me with a crooked finger and asked me what I was doing. When I explained that I was trying to lighten up the place, he told me not to do that. He explained that he had constructed the building and the company culture in a certain way for a reason, professionalism. I understood the reason for professionalism, but I think that people have a right to enjoy their jobs and each other, too. Facilitative leaders enjoy work and those they work with.

I had another experience telling the pig with a peg leg story on a business trip to Holland. On the last evening prior to leaving Holland, a colleague and I visited a quaint bar. Everyone was very nice to us, speaking in English so we could understand their conversations. A gentleman named Bob, who arrived halfway through the night, was quite a storyteller. His jokes and stories were flying fast and furiously. Everyone seemed to enjoy his humor. As the night wore on, I decided to tell my favorite story, of the pig with the peg leg. As I got into the story, every time I said the word peg leg, all of the listeners looked away rather embarrassedly. I began to worry that peg leg was a dirty phrase in Dutch. I looked at Bob and asked, "You know what a peg leg is, don't you?" Bob looked at me sternly. He grabbed his right leg, threw it up on the bar, and said, "Yeah, I've got one." I stared at his leg in horror and then reached over and felt it. Sure enough, it was hard as a rock. The blood drained from my face, and I felt faint. Suddenly, Bob and everyone else burst into laughter. The joke was on me. Bob wasn't offended; in fact, he loved my story. For the rest of the evening, when any group of people he knew came in, he would hurry over to them and tell the story of me telling my story. I could see him pointing at me and again everyone would break into laughter. I learned that communication and humor that work well in one situation can be clumsy in another situation.

Leadership and Change

A few years ago I spent nine days rafting the Colorado River through the Grand Canyon with my two brothers. During this trip I interviewed several of the commercial raft guides about the leadership behaviors of successful boatmen. The word that I heard most often to describe leadership was flexibility. The boatmen described the ability to deal with a number of complex and rapidly developing situations and the differing personalities of customers and peers.

In the summer of 1997, I visited an archaeological dig north of Springfield, Missouri, where my brother, Jack, was supervising a crew who was excavating the site. The area was being eroded by the Sac River with the aid of the periodic release of water from a hydroelectric dam upstream. Six feet of water were flushed down this stream within moments several times a week to meet the electric power needs of Kansas City, Missouri. Ten thousand years of data were being destroyed every week. This dramatic erosion had created a twenty foot cliff from the top of the terrace to the stream bed.

One day during my visit Jack and I took a canoe trip on the upper Sac River, setting out on the river just below the dam. Carl, one of Jack's staff members, stayed behind to hinder local arrowhead hunters from looting the site. While we were gone, an interesting event occurred. Adjoining the fenced-off site was a cattle farm. A three hundred and fifty pound calf that was blind in both eyes had accidentally fallen off the cliff into the stream bed. Carl realized that he could not help the calf by himself. The calf would be in jeopardy if an unscheduled flood occurred. After a while, a couple of fishermen floated down the river and sighted the calf. Carl and the two fishermen gave of their time and energy to save the calf. Carl pulled on a rope tied around the calf's neck. The fishermen pushed and lifted the calf up this steep bank. Once they reached the top of the cliff, Carl suggested that they leave the rope on the calf and lead him through the gate. Carl left to open the gate, and the fishermen decided that leading the calf was more difficult than shooing him through the gate. They took the rope off the calf and started yelling and waving their arms. The blind calf, scared by the sounds, ran in the other direction, right back over the cliff again.

The moral of the story is that you have to fit your leadership style to your followers. The approach of the fishermen would have worked well with a sighted calf. It was unsuccessful with a blind calf. The fishermen were facilitative with the donation of their time and energy. However, they did not consider the unique characteristics of this calf. Leaders have to be flexible with their leadership styles. The leadership style has to fit the skills, abilities, and characteristics of the followers. By the way, the calf's mother kept us all awake that night calling for the blind calf. The next day the calf's mother led him up the river to a spot where he could make it back up the bank, and he was saved. She knew the leadership style that would work given the calf's disability.

Chaos and Leadership

Because of the myriad of changes imposed upon organizations recently, many speak of their organizations as immersed in chaos. I suggest that we will never eliminate chaos, only learn to structure it to some extent. When I worked in the coal mine, we were periodically required to walk the intake escapeway so that everyone knew how to get out in the event of an emergency. Some of the escapeways were in low top, which is a ceiling or roof less than five feet in height. Sometimes we would walk several miles in these low areas. Years and months before, when the escapeway was being mined, the first layer of stone would occasionally fall in. These areas were supported and ended up being six or seven feet in height. During the walk out of the escapeway when we reached these fall areas, we would all stand up to stretch our backs before continuing the walk through the low top. The miners called these areas "glory holes." Many of my clients are looking for glory holes to rest from the chaos of their organizational environment. Unfortunately, I believe that the glory holes in the chaos will be fewer and farther between in the future.

Many companies are seeking radical ways of surviving and succeeding given the state of persistent change. Jack Welch, CEO of the General Electric Company, proposes a process called "work out" to deal with these change issues. Team members get together for a dedicated period of time to reinvent the way work is accomplished. Jack Welch's leadership philosophy of a modern, multinational corporation has been both criticized and praised (Slater, 1993; Tichy & Sherman, 1993). However, no one can deny that Welch's leadership is a vibrant attempt to address today's competitive environment and demanding customer needs. One of the results of Welch's leadership is a perception of organizational chaos at all levels.

Margaret Wheatley (1992) proposes that chaos is natural, flexible, and self-organizing. She uses chaos illustrations, such as clouds and streams, to suggest that we must not resist chaos but rather view it as a natural evolutionary state for an organization in transition. Wheatley agrees with the humanist theorists rather than with the mechanistic view that organizations can be compared to a machine and can be dissected, analyzed, and put back together in an improved form. Wheatley proposes that each organization is unique because of the diversity of its people, products, and external forces. There is a perceived element of chaos in each of them. She makes three suggestions for dealing with this chaos. First, focus on the information as the primary organizing force. Rather than using information as power, we need to use information to organize work. While at BorgWarner Chemicals, I facilitated sessions with all nonexempt and hourly employees where new types of information were shared for the first time. Previously the information we discussed had only been available at the vice president's level. Items involved productivity, profitability, new products, and plans for new foreign plants. Different vice presidents appeared before the plant operators to present this information and answer questions. This approach was significant for BorgWarner Chemicals. They were dramatically moving from a need-to-know basis to a why-not-tell-them posture. The results were more understanding of the business and broader employee ownership.

Second, realize that relationships define reality in organizations. Organizational members need to be free to seek out and access others in the organization. In one organization where I have spent some time, employees had to get permission from their managers prior to asking questions of or talking about business with employees from another department. Usually, the supervisor would take the question or information to the manager of the other department who would then approach his or her employee. The return path of the response took a similar route. Of course, this communication process creates many misunderstandings. I asked the question, "How would it hurt the organization if employees were allowed to communicate freely in any direction the business required?" The answer was, "Employees would make decisions and when managers were asked about them in a meeting, they would be embarrassed by their ignorance of the issue." I suggested that decisions should be made at the lowest level possible. In order to keep managers informed of critical decisions, those types of decisions could be identified and e-mail messages written for timely updating. Leveraging employee intellect and decision making creates a powerful synergy.

Finally, see vision as an energy field. Energy fields can be almost nonexistent, or they can be strong drivers for organizational success. Take, for example, President Kennedy's declaration in 1961 that we, as a country, would send men safely to the moon and back by the end of the century. Most of us didn't believe it was possible. Later, an attitude almost like an energy field was created, and the impossible became reality. Action that leads toward a vision is the result of consistent verbal and nonverbal messages from leaders.

Leadership Emergence

While growing up, I was involved in 4-H, which is a rural youth organization. My projects were the showing of Jersey cattle at the county fair. One of my grand champion cows was September Morn. She was ranged on a sixty-acre farm with a mixed breed Guernsey named Rose. Every morning I would find the two cows in the barnyard patiently waiting to be milked. At the time of this story, September Morn was ready to calf any day. One summer morning, I arrived at the barnyard to the frantic bellowing of Rose. September Morn was nowhere to be seen. She had never been absent before and Rose's behavior was also unusual. I entered the field, and Rose immediately took off in the opposite direction. I followed her almost half a mile to the other side of the farm. There I found September Morn lying on a hillside that had a gentle slope. She had delivered her calf the night before, and the calf had rolled down the hill. I picked up the calf, and September Morn got up and followed me. I carried the calf home and both were fine.

Rose had always been the follower of September Morn. This day, however, she took an important leadership role. I learned from this experience that leadership often arises from unexpected sources. It is important that we are aware of this fact. We need to encourage all employees to express their leadership abilities. People will surprise us.

Modes of Facilitative Leadership

The facilitative leader functions in a number of different modes. The following six chapters discuss five effective modes: enabler of change, respectful communicator, developer of people and teams, master of problem-solving tools, and manager of conflict. An enabler of change sets the organization's vision and communicates the reasons and purposes for change to all employees. He or she sees the leader's job as helping all organizational members understand the business needs and obtain the proper tools to be successful in their changing business environment. The respectful communicator talks in the language of the people who are listening, taking care that the message is understandable and understood. The developer of people and teams believes in the potential of all employees and invests organizational resources to improve their skills. As a master of problem-solving tools, the facilitative leader thinks in terms of systematically improving a situation, identifying appropriate problem-solving tools, and teaching these tools to all employees. The facilitative leader also models these tools in everyday problem-solving activities. Finally, the facilitative leader is a manager of conflict, dealing with the root of interpersonal conflict and discussing the communication culture of the organization to illustrate the conflict and to find a means of resolution. Effective use of feedback is also critically involved in the facilitative leader's conflict management.

This book focuses on the concept of the facilitative leader. However, I suggest that the behaviors we will explore are appropriate for all organizational members.

Summary

This chapter defined the concept of leadership and the evolution of leadership theory and structures in this century. Common leadership behaviors were identified and described. In addition, several stories that illustrate various aspects of the facilitative leader were related. Finally, the five leadership modes that make up the core of this book were previewed.

Questions from Chapter 1

1. How did Taylor's approach to organizational structure relate to employee commitment?
2. How did the Hawthorne studies initiate the Human Relations movement?
3. What findings linked the Iowa, Ohio State, and Michigan studies?
4. How do the various organization development initiatives of the past two decades, sometimes called fads, relate to one another?
5. Define what continuous performance improvement means for today's organization.
   A. How is it different from past expectations?
   B. How does the facilitative leader deal with continuous performance improvement?
6. How is humor related to leadership?
7. Define the changes you have experienced in the last five years. How have you responded to these changes?

Actions from Chapter 1

1. List the behaviors of the best leader you have known personally. Prioritize these behaviors in terms of importance. Select the most important two behaviors that you presently don't exhibit and practice them.

2. Write down the vision of your organization. If there are parts of this vision that you don't understand, seek a knowledgeable person and ask the appropriate questions.

3. Describe how your leadership behaviors relate to the five modes of the facilitative leader. Choose the most important area on which you should focus.

Enabler of Change

Enabler Definition

The facilitative leader is an enabler of change who assists employees and helps them with the change process, recognizing when to hand the ball off to organizational members. Bass (1990) describes leaders as agents of change "whose acts affect other people more than other people's acts affect them" (pp. 19–20). Block (1981) describes the element of authenticity (being genuine or real) as the single most important characteristic of a successful change enabler. The word *enabler* is appropriate because the facilitative leader uses influence rather than direct power to make changes or implement programs. The connotation of the word *enabler* in the health care field, especially among drug abuse counselors, is negative. It means one who allows another to continue to use drugs. My use of the word is extremely positive. *Funk & Wagnall's New Encyclopedia* (1996) defines *enable* as "to supply with means, knowledge, or opportunity." This is the definition I use throughout the book.

Every day, we choose to change. In the last year, how many of you have chosen to take a new job or responsibility, entered or exited a relationship, moved, or had a child? These are all significant changes which, for the most part, we willingly chose. We evaluate different choices in our lives and select the alternative that makes the most sense to us.

Many leaders expect that their employees will automatically realize the need for change and do the "right thing." As we well know, this adoption of change initiatives does not occur easily or quickly. On the other hand, there are many examples of organizations that have strategically raised their employees' awareness of the need for change and in which behaviors have in fact changed.

All individuals in organizations make decisions to support, fight, or ignore organizational decisions and initiatives. We make choices; others make decisions that impact our choices. Employee or team member commitment is not guaranteed; certain critical factors must be addressed to create this commitment. Think about the times in your life when someone else tried to force you to do something without adequate explanation of the reasons the action should be taken. How much energy did you expend? For me, the energy output was low in those situations.

Maurer (1996) describes resistance as having three levels. The first level involves resistance to the idea itself. This resistance may result from lack of understanding or a desire to maintain the status quo. An example of level 1 resistance I've encountered was the introduction of a new performance appraisal system. Once the organizational needs and benefits of the new performance appraisal system were described in a training session, much of the resistance subsided.

Level 2 resistance involves deeper issues. Often this resistance results from unspoken issues such as trust and respect. In one organization the introduction of teams was met with level 2 resistance. Supervisors felt the initiative was designed to reduce their status and eliminate their jobs. Operators believed the change would result in more work for them and being held accountable unfairly for things outside their control. Downsizing was also a concern of theirs. Open communication sessions to hear their issues and plan to avoid negative outcomes for individuals involved were held. Venting occurred but soon resolutions were reached that were satisfactory for all parties.

Level 3 resistance is more deeply embedded and involves more historic animosity or conflicting values and vision. While I was facilitating a discussion with a group of chemical operators in 1986 on the success of some Japanese management processes, one gentleman stood up and said, "I didn't surrender to the Japs [sic] in 1944, and I am not going to now." Of course this was difficult to deal with. I expressed an understanding of his feelings and turned to the other participants to gather their feelings on the changes the plant management was proposing. Most of them agreed that the movement toward more employee involvement was positive in their minds. When the resistance is this emotional, it is best not to engage in an argument but rather to test the perceptions of others involved. If there is consensus on the level 3 emotion, considerable dialogue is required over time to address the issue. It could be possible given a volume of this type of resistance that the initiative may not be right with this population or at this time.

You Can't Push a Pig into a Truck

Let me tell you a story that illustrates how we effectively choose to make changes in our lives (Ray, 1997). I grew up on a small farm in Southeastern Ohio. My father always kept at least one pig on the farm. Periodically, my father decided that it was time to take our sow to a neighboring farm for a social visit with our neighbor's boar. One warm summer day, my father announced to my brother and me that it was time for this semiannual visit. He asked us to load the pig into the truck while he took care of some other chores. We proceeded to place the ramp onto the back of the truck, and the pig curiously started up the ramp. Just as curiously, however, the pig stopped on the ramp and looked around. Fearing that her next step would be back down the ramp and that we would lose all the territory she had given us freely, my brother and I took action. We each placed a shoulder against the rump of the pig and attempted to push the pig into the truck. As anyone who has had experience with pigs will realize, this approach was doomed to failure.

The pig, who weighed more than my brother and me together soaking wet, backed up when she felt us pushing, flinging us into mud puddles on each side of the ramp. At that very moment, our father turned the corner of the barn in time to observe our misfortune. He was greatly amused by our plight. Once his laughter subsided, he admonished us both with, "Boys, I taught you how to load a pig and that's not the way to do it." He proceeded to the barn and returned with a small metal cup of shelled corn. He then lined a Hansel and

DRAWING BY AUDREY TATUM

Gretel–like trail of corn up the ramp and threw the rest into the truck. In three minutes, the pig was loaded and happy to be there.

Recently, as I thought about the problems of leading organizations and employee commitment, this story came to mind. I realized that it had significant application to the process of organizational change. Like the pig that willingly entered the truck once she realized it was in her own interest (the joy of eating corn), if people know how any change effort will help them personally, they can make objective decisions. You can't push a pig into a truck. However, a pig will choose to go where it believes its needs will be met.

Example of Change Enabler

At BorgWarner Chemicals, anytime a major change occurred, the plant manager would institute small group meetings to explain the reasons for the change and the benefits and challenges for the company and the employees. This is one example of a facilitative leader enabling change among organizational members.

The Demographics of Change

In working with a variety of organizations, I have found that there are at least three different groups of people who respond to change in consistent ways. I call this distribution the demographics of change.

The first group is the Change Champions, the people who have a thirst for learning. They have a regular reading schedule in addition to the local newspaper. They read professional journals and popular organizational change and leadership books. They are constantly thinking about how to help the organization be successful. Generally, this group constitutes about 10 to 20 percent of the organization's population.

DRAWING BY JENIFER HALSTEAD

FIGURE 2-1. THE DEMOGRAPHICS OF CHANGE

On the other side of the spectrum is a group I call the "Hell, no, we won't go" group, people who look upon change as a hurtful experience. Their first response to change is, "How will this change hurt me? How am I going to get screwed this time? What do I need to do to stop this?" You can visually spot members of this group by looking at their shoes. Their heels are worn away at a 45-degree angle from being dragged into the future. They also tend to leave two black marks on the linoleum as they attempt to resist. The size of this group is generally about equal to that of the change champions, 10 to 20 percent.

The largest group in most organizations is made up of the Fence Sitters, 60 to 80 percent of the total population. This group of employees prefer to let others test the waters of change initiation or resistance. However, they are active observers of the success or failure of the two other groups. If the change champions are successful, rewarded, and having fun, the Fence Sitters start moving in that direction. When movement occurs in this direction, real organizational change occurs. If the "Hell, no, we won't go" group is surviving and thriving, the Fence Sitters may move in the direction of resisting the change effort. When this decision is made by the majority of the Fence Sitters, there is a tidal wave of change resistance in the organization, and the change effort is perceived as "flavor of the month" or just another fad. All members of all three groups are making decisions about what is good for the organization and for themselves personally. I have also found that depending upon the issue, I have been a member of each group.

The facilitative leader deals with members of each group differently. My motto is to work with the willing, usually the Change Champions. Change Champions must have an opportunity to hear about and ask questions about the vision. They also must be rewarded for success in accomplishing the vision. It must be clear to all organizational members what the desired behaviors are and what the rewards are for individuals who are successful in demonstrating these behaviors. The Fence Sitters are a critical population and must not be ignored. Opportunities for employees to move from the Fence Sitters' camp to the Change Champions' camp must be made available. The more success around the new behaviors that is observed, the more movement you will see in the desired direction. The "Hell, no, we won't go" group is often the most frustrating group. It is important to remember that these people are not bad people or bad employees. In fact, I have at times seen this group become the core of the Change Champions. Tremendous energy and conviction of rightness exist within members of this group. They are looking for concrete evidence that the new initiative is different from past, failed initiatives. They also want others to listen to and pay attention to them. Sometimes, when a facilitative leader simply listens to their concerns and describes the relationship of the concerns to the proposed behavioral changes, the resistant group members choose to change. In contrast, it is important not to let a minority of the organization stop significant, needed change. Communicate, communicate, and communicate, but don't forget to make things happen. Facilitative leaders lose credibility when they communicate but nothing happens. Remember, actions speak louder than words. We will spend more time on this issue in Chapter 3.

The Vertical Turtle

Another story illustrates the role of the facilitative leader as an enabler of change. One day, after a four-inch deluge of rain, I decided to inspect a nearby creek along which I had often hiked. As I approached the mouth of the creek, I saw flattened grass above the stream. The water was flowing in channels that only hours previously had been dry. I continued up the stream, walking in the water where a path usually led. The whole creek bottom had been covered in the torrent. Everything was new and changed.

DRAWING BY AUDREY TATUM

Suddenly, in the distance, I saw a blur of yellow. When I got closer, I realized it was a box turtle that was stuck in the mud. In the midst of the rare chaos that had engulfed this small valley, the storm swept the turtle out of its safe refuge under a pile of leaves at the top of the hill. Along with rocks, mud, leaves, and sticks, the turtle was hurled down the hillside. Once the water resided, the turtle found itself stuck fast in a solid mud pit. Only its head and front legs were visible. I looked at it for a few moments and then stuck my walking stick behind its shell and popped it out. I rinsed the turtle off in the creek and then set it on the bank. Eventually, off it ambled.

The turtle's experience reminded me of the chaos and change with which many of my clients struggle daily. The catastrophic change had unexpectedly snatched the turtle out of its comfort zone and thrust it into a new, unique experience. Organizational members are similarly thrown to and fro constantly. My role in the turtle's life was as a change enabler; I helped it survive a catastrophic event. I believe that we should look for opportunities to be change enablers with subordinates, peers, and other organizational members. Change enabling is one of the modes of the facilitative leader.

Risk Taker

The facilitative leader acts as a risk taker, learning from and willingly allowing others to learn from mistakes. Many people agree that the most significant learning in life results from mistakes they have experienced. I know this source of learning has been valuable for me. One manager who was talking with his new employees for the first time expressed an interesting philosophy. To use a baseball metaphor, he insisted that he didn't want players who batted 1000. He also didn't want players with a 100 batting average. Players who bat 1000 never step out and swing at the difficult issues. Safety is their rule of action. Players who bat at 100 are not skillful enough to enable the success of the team. The figure that he suggested was an ambitious batting average of 600 to 800.

Let's go back to our friend, the vertical turtle. During the two weeks after I had encountered the vertical turtle, I found myself telling its story many times. I told it to clients, family, and friends. As I often do, I became enamored of the story. I also found that I became curious about the fate of the unfortunate turtle. Finally, I ventured back to the location where I had found the vertical turtle. Just before I reached the now dry patch of mud that had encased the turtle, I started to step over a small tributary when I looked down to my left. There, to my surprise, was my buddy, the vertical turtle, in another serious mess. This time it was desperately trying to extricate itself from a sheer, slippery sloped pool of water. This watery grave was a plunge pool newly carved by the recent torrent of rain that had hurled the turtle down the hillside. It was soon apparent that the turtle was not going to be able to get out on its own. When its energy ran out, its fate was to eventually drown. Once again, I came to the turtle's rescue by plucking it from the water.

DRAWING BY AUDREY TATUM

At first I thought, "Is this turtle stupid!" Later, I thought better of the event. Everyday life can be confusing. Two mistakes are entirely possible even for people with the highest competence and the most excellent intentions. The facilitative leader must have patience and persistence when leading organizational members. Be clear with directions and focus most of your communication on how to succeed in the future, rather than on what went wrong in the past. Learn from your failures and allow others to do the same. Risk taking is seldom demonstrated in those organizations where the rule is one strike and you're out.

Facilitative leaders must view risk taking as a positive learning event. Taking risks enables others to invent ways of successfully surviving change. Learning from failures increases our worth as employees because we are less likely to repeat that mistake. Also, facilitative leaders should establish relationships with those who have had success demonstrating desired skills. Work relationships should be seen as learning opportunities.

Feelings about Change

Several other insights concerning change occurred to me during a recent trip to Costa Rica. My brother and I had traveled there to see the country and do some rafting. We were less than twenty-five minutes from San Jose when the pilot of our flight came on the loudspeaker to address the passengers. He said, "Folks, I have some bad news." (I don't know about you, but that is not a phrase I like to hear from the pilot who is flying my plane.) He went on to explain, "We have just gotten word that the San Jose airport has been closed. Right now we don't know if it will be closed for twenty-four minutes or twenty-four hours. But we have plenty of fuel, so we'll just circle for a little bit until we find out what's happening." At this point the communication among the passengers changed. It was as if we had momentarily become best friends. Everyone realized that we were in the same boat, literally.

After a short time, the pilot again came on the loudspeaker and said, "We just heard from San Jose that the airport will be closed for twenty-four hours. We don't know where we can land yet, but our people on the ground are working on it. Our choices are Managua, Nicaragua and Panama City, Panama. We'll let you know as soon as we find out." My confidence was not increasing at this point. Finally, we got word that we had permission to land at Panama City. However, the unexpected changes were not over for the night. We still had to survive two lengthy taxi rides and a two-hour wait in line at a hotel.

I realized a key point about change from this experience. First, sometimes change impacts us, and we have no choice. In those situations, however, we do have a choice about how we react to the change. My brother was depressed about losing a day of vacation in Costa Rica. But I had never been to Panama, so I was excited to be visiting another country.

Learning from Experienced People

We finally reached Costa Rica about noon on the following day. We rented a four-wheel-drive vehicle and headed northeast into the mountains, where the best white-water rivers are located. The roads were terrible, so it was after dark before we got to our hotel. It rained almost ten inches that night. The sound on our hotel's tin roof lulled us to sleep. The next day, we headed to see a raft outfitter we had been referred to, and by early afternoon we were on the Sarapique River. It turned out that this river was more of a challenge than we expected. We were told that the river's gradient was about 18 feet per mile. Instead, the first 5 miles dropped at approximately 80 feet per mile. After thirty minutes of constant rapids, I was whipped and drained. With two miles of serious rapids to go, I was thrown into the air, and, when I came back down, the raft wasn't under me. Luckily, I held onto my paddle and grabbed the rope on the side of the raft as I came down. My brother immediately moved to my aid, since he knew that this was a life-threatening situation. He grabbed me by my life jacket-but wasn't braced enough to help me back into the raft. He braced himself and jerked all 212 pounds of me back into the raft. After my brother's first failure to get me back into the raft, the guide was making his way to the front of the raft to lend a hand. When he left his rudder position, the raft was thrown into a hole, or hydraulic, as boatmen call them. All we could do was lie across the raft, anchor our feet on the far side, and dig our paddles into the surf to keep the raft from tipping. The guide attempted several maneuvers to pop us out of the hole until he was exhausted. Finally, he frantically waved to our fifteen-year-old safety kayaker to make his way up the shore rocks and throw us a safety rope. The kayaker finally did so, missing us wide right with his first throw. Our energy was draining minute by minute. The safety kayaker missed us wide left with his second throw. I wasn't sure I could hold on for another throw. Prior to the third throw, our guide, David, handed me his paddle and dove for the rope, successfully. We were pulled out of the hole in a matter of seconds.

I realized two more key points about change from this experience. First, when attempting a new change experience, find someone who has already done it or something similar to it before and question him or her carefully about the situation. Pay attention, and learn from this person. Second, once you make the decision to commit to a change, give it all you have.

Definer of Vision

The definition of the organizational vision is the primary responsibility of the facilitative leader and an important step in enabling organizational members to change. The leader senses the environment, assesses the strengths and concerns of organizational members, and points out the direction for the future. The facilitative leader senses the external environment through association in professional organizations, reading, and benchmarking. Some well-known professional organizations that may assist facilitative leaders are the American Society for Training and Development, the Association for Quality and Participation, the Society for Human Resource Management, and the American Society of Quality Control. These associations have many local affiliated organizations. Another environmental sensing technique is to have a consistent reading regime. Start with professional journals and then set a goal to read a book a month. Choose books that relate to the state-of-the-art organization that you desire to develop and lead. A third means of staying up with the current of organizational change is benchmarking. "Benchmarking means comparing oneself to an objective standard, such as a competitor's performance." (Tichy & Sherman, 1993, p. 249). Identify other organizations that are successful in inventing new ways of accomplishing organizational work. These organizations can be suppliers, customers, neighboring companies, or companies that have been documented in the literature. Don't limit your benchmarking to companies in your own industry. Some of the most significant learning can come from outside your industry. Talk with members of these organizations, or better yet, visit them. Some of the most valuable motivation can result from sending organizational members from all levels to visit benchmark organizations. By doing this type of benchmarking, you can create exciting, positive organizational stories.

It is also possible to start your own benchmarking network. After the Bhopal disaster in India in 1984, the potential liability and community impact of poor operator training were on the minds of many people in the chemical industry. In response to my concerns, I invited my peer trainers from all of the chemical companies in a hundred-mile radius of my site for a benchmarking session. Over a two-year period, we met at every trainer's site to see their training facilities and to learn about their technical training systems. I also established an intraorganizational network of my peers from all sites within my company. My purpose was to learn about their training activities and to share my knowledge from the interorganizational group. I know of several similar networks, such as regular meetings of local plant managers. Some networks hire professional coordinators to take care of logistics for the group. To start your own group, identify a group of people from whom you would like to learn. Structure an agenda that is open, yet gives potential attendees an idea of the nature of the meeting. Then send invitations. End each meeting with a listing of key points learned by attendees. Sharing key learnings is a facilitated technique to document significant points that were shared in the session.

Another means of assessing the environment is called a SWOT analysis, focusing on the organization's Strengths, Weaknesses, Opportunities, and Threats. Either individually or with a group, discuss these variables as they relate to your company. When you have this discussion, the drivers and barriers to your organization will be documented. Ask each of the following four questions twice, once for issues external to the organization and once for issues internal to the organization:

1.   What are the organization's present strengths?
2.   What are the organization's present weaknesses?
3.   What are the organization's future opportunities?
4.   What are the organization's future threats?

Each of us has a vision of how to do our job and how to improve our job performance. Many of us, however, don't talk often to others about this vision. Sit down right now and jot down where you would like to be or what you would like to know in five years. This is your vision for yourself. Now think about your job and go through the same visioning process. Visions are moving targets of sorts. They have to be updated constantly. When I was a union miner in the early 70s, I believed that the top managers of the mine knew the best way to run the mine for its future success. However, what I saw and what they told me didn't seem to be a complete picture. I thought that they were just feeding me what they thought I needed to know. Later, when I was promoted to section supervisor, I had more opportunity to talk with the top managers, and I became more aware of exactly what they wanted to see happen. The whys behind their vision were clearer. I was surprised that they didn't have all the answers and even involved me in the planning. Later, when I was hired as a plant training manager, I was deeply involved in developing the vision and the action steps to implement it. My input was specifically solicited during development meetings, and I was one of the critical players who communicated and discussed the vision with all employees through various training and planning sessions.

Finally, I assumed the role of corporate training director for a billion-dollar company. The daily decisions that reflected the company's vision were more fluid than I had ever expected. I realized that there was no perfect template for the organization. Top managers were assessing the best data available and constantly redesigning the vision to meet business needs.

The point here is that it is difficult for organizational members to understand the visioning process of their leaders since they have never been in the leaders' shoes. Therefore, it is important for the facilitative leader to explain as much as possible about the background and drivers of the vision. Just communicating the vision is not enough. The leader must give detailed information on the whys behind the vision. Spending time discussing the vision with organizational members and answering questions results in member commitment to the vision.

Communicating the Vision

You never arrive at having completed your vision. If you're effective in your visioning, you will change the vision before you reach it! I believe that if the vision is presented, discussed, and planned for comprehensively, people will choose to make the vision reality. The problem with this change process is that it takes precious time. Leaders of large organizations often find a cascading approach useful in communicating and discussing the vision. First, the facilitative leader presents a vision. Then, the immediate facilitative leader of the group facilitates a dialogue regarding the concerns and positive impressions of the team members. There is no magic solution other than talking to people repeatedly about needed changes. I call this face time. One of the reasons that people higher in the organization understand and buy into any vision is that they spend more time together discussing the vision, the needs for the vision, and the plans for making the vision reality. It is expensive but very important that all employees be given repeated time to discuss the vision.

When working with a management team to define an organization's vision, I often warm up the group with an exercise that I call cultural definers. I employ the six variables that Schein (1992) used to define organizational culture. These variables are the *behaviors* that are observed in organizations, the *norms* that are supported by organizational members, the *values* espoused by the organization, the *philosophy* that guides the organization's policy toward employees and customers, the *rules* that help employees to fit into the organization, and the feeling or *climate* of the organization. I ask the team to describe their present organization using these variables and give it a nickname of a wild animal, such as an elephant because of its size, a jack rabbit because of its erratic movement, or an ostrich because it hides from the tough issues. Next, I ask the team members to choose a nickname for the future desired organization, using the same six variables. Some people choose the eagle because of its all-encompassing view of the lay of the land. Others select a flock of geese because of its team alignment while flying and the trading of the leadership role by flock members. Still others identify the giraffe because of its ability to look over the everyday fray and see the bigger picture. This exercise has been useful in getting organizational members to open group communication and think about common future goals.

Change is, by definition, movement from one set of behaviors to a new set of behaviors. When working with a team on change issues, the next discussion should begin with a review of the key responsibilities and behaviors that are demonstrated every day. In two groups, have the team construct a list by brainstorming their present behaviors and responsibilities. It is always interesting to see the degree of alignment or agreement between the two groups. Next, bring the two groups together to compare the lists. Eliminate any duplications that appear on both lists. Finally, prioritize the combined list.

Often, organizational members feel that their roles in the organization are not valued. The exercise on role and behavior definition helps workers and management reinforce the importance of each worker's role. An operator in a chemical plant told me frankly that his supervisor expected him to "check his brain at the gate and rent his hands for eight hours." Most people would view this interaction as disrespectful, a perception that is not unfounded. As a machine operator in the coal mine, I once recommended to my section supervisor a particular course of action regarding the use of my roof bolting machine. He walked up close to me, grinning and exclaiming, "You've got one boss, and you're looking at him." He then walked away with no further discussion. I felt disrespected and embarrassed. The result of this exchange was that in the future, I kept my ideas to myself. Certainly, this is not the desired result for today's organizations.

Next, the facilitative leader should turn the discussion to the organizational vision, checking with the team members to determine their support for the direction. Then the team needs to identify and examine desired future behaviors that will be needed if the vision is to be accomplished. To gather these thoughts, split the team into two groups to construct the list of roles and behaviors needed in the future. Repeat the consolidation and prioritization process.

The Change Model

Now that both present and future behaviors have been identified, the gap between the two sets of behaviors needs to be clarified. The formula for this exercise is FB − PB = GB (future behaviors minus present

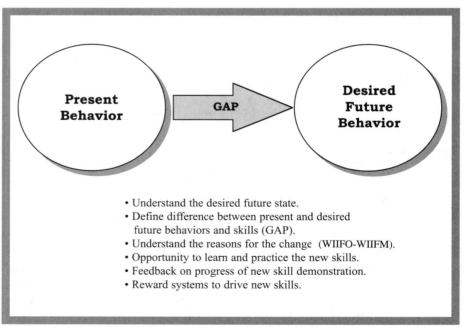

FIGURE 2-2. THE CHANGE MODEL

behaviors equals gap behaviors). The gap behaviors are critical to the change process. By defining the gap behaviors, all parties involved can focus on developing the unique, new behavior.

For example, some future behaviors could be:

Operators need to run the equipment consistently.

Operators need to be on time to relieve the previous shift operator.

Operators need to be able to communicate respectfully with one another.

Operators need to solve problems as a group.

Operators need to address conflict in a timely and effective manner.

Operators need to brief the incoming operators on the events during our shift.

Some present behaviors could be:

Operators need to present problems to the supervisor to be solved.

Operators need to hand conflict situations over to the supervisor to solve.

Operators need to run the equipment consistently.

Operators need to be on time to relieve the previous shift operator.

Operators need to brief the incoming operators on the events during our shift.

As we can see, communicating respectfully, solving problems as a group, and dealing with conflict interpersonally are areas where the group needs to improve skill sets to enable successful change to be accomplished.

Once the gap is clarified, the need for the change must be conveyed. A dual-focused Why Change? exercise is useful to consolidate people's thinking about change. First, pose the question, "What does your organization expect to gain from instituting this change?" I call this first phase WIIFO (What's in it for the organization?). When the proposed change is a move to advance from traditional work structures to team interactions, many group members respond with comments such as:

They want to improve customer service.

They want to save money.

They expect people will be more committed.

They will be able to do more with less.

They expect that quality will improve.

They expect waste to decrease.

They expect productivity to increase.

The second phase is called WIIFM (What's in it for me?). Although responses to this question vary based upon the change issue involved, the following comments are common:

I will have more job security.

I will have more say in my job.

Work will be more interesting.

I will be treated with more respect.

Once group members understand the reasons for the change, the organization has an ethical responsibility to give employees opportunities to develop the new desired skills. This can consist of formal training from external or internal programs, coaching by the leader, coaching by peers or other organizational members, assigned reading material, computer based instruction, or a combination of any or all of the above approaches. Regardless of the approach used, it is important to continue to assess with the employee whether or not the new skill has been mastered.

Two other requirements remain. First, the organizational leaders at all levels must give continual feedback on how well employees are succeeding on the gap behaviors. Second, reward systems must be in place that reinforce the new desired behaviors rather than past behaviors. In fact, the reward system should focus on the behaviors needed five or ten years in the future. Unfortunately, many organizations are still rewarding desired behaviors of the 1960s or 1970s.

Change Model Questions

1. What behaviors are presently expected regarding this situation?
2. What behaviors will be expected in the future?
3. What are the new behaviors (GAP) that will be expected in the future?

4. How will these changes help the company?

5. How will these changes help each individual?

6. How can we create an opportunity for individuals to learn the required new behaviors?

7. How can I structure time to give feedback on an individual's progress in learning and demonstrating the new skills?

8. How can I reward individuals for achieving the new skills?

9. What else do I need to know to be able to effectively communicate about this change?

Summary

In this chapter we explained the concept of change enabler that is central to the nature of the facilitative leader. The relationship between choice and ownership of a selected alternative was illustrated with a story. The demographics of change describe the different ways we respond to change in our lives. The need for organizational members to help one another survive today's change was highlighted. Also, the importance of allowing people to learn from risk taking was expressed. Finally, the steps of the change model were detailed. First, elements of the visioning process are identified. Second, the present and future desired behaviors are discussed. Third, the whys of the change are explored with the WIIFO-WIIFM exercise. Other components needed to accomplish real organizational change are an opportunity to learn the skills, feedback on new skill acquisition, and rewards for demonstrating the desired skills.

Questions from Chapter 2

1. In the last year, what changes have you freely chosen to make?

2. How do the above changes contrast to the ones that have been forced upon you by others?

3. What information would have been helpful to enable you to support these changes?

4. During recent change initiatives, in which category did you find yourself most often?

    A. Change champion (Seeking and supporting change initiatives)

    B. Fence sitter (Waiting to see impact of change initiatives)

    C. Hell, no, we won't go (Actively resisting change initiatives)

5. How can you help others survive the change initiatives they are experiencing?

Actions from Chapter 2

1. Choose a change goal for yourself. Identify a person who has accomplished a similar goal. Contact this person and talk about how he or she was successful in attaining the goal.

2. Identify another organization that is innovative and state-of-the art. Visit this organization and take notes on the techniques, processes, and systems they have in place. Also share with them your change learnings.

3. Identify where you would like to be five years from now.

    A. Desired job.

    B. New skills.

    C. Personal goals.

    D. Completed experiences.

4. Define specific steps that will enable you to accomplish this vision.

5. Set time frames for accomplishing each step of this vision.

3

Respectful Communicator

"What we have here is a failure to communicate." Does that sound like individuals with whom you work, or an old Paul Newman movie? At times we have all heard people say, "You're not listening to me"; "The only way I find out anything is through the grapevine"; or "I have to scream before you pay attention to me." These complaints are all symptoms of poor interpersonal communication practices.

The facilitative leader demonstrates respectful communication when talking with other organizational members. We can all become more facilitative communicators through processes such as training and coaching. One step is to increase our awareness of how and why we communicate the way we do. Another important step is to identify new communication behaviors to practice.

The Field of Experience and Shared Understanding

Let's look at how we communicate. We each have a set of words and nonverbal movements with which we are comfortable. We'll call these words and nonverbal movements *symbols*. Most of our communication uses these symbols. We are sensory animals. We are constantly processing and interpreting stimuli such as smells, sights, tastes, touch, and sounds. As we become aware of these stimuli, we filter them through our past experience. We then attach meaning to the stimuli and choose a response. Finally, we send the communication by speaking or by nonverbal movement.

Next let's examine why we communicate the way we do. How did we develop our communication skills? Were we born with them or did we learn them? Schramm (1954) maintained that we learn how to communicate through every experience we have, thus creating a field of experience. If you observe small children, you will probably see them imitating those around them. This imitation is a demonstration of how we develop our field of experience. We learn our communication skills by watching those around us. We use many of the same words that Mom and Dad did. We smile like Dad or speak quickly like Mom. As we observe others, we experiment with new behaviors, repeating those that work well. If we have no alternative behaviors available, we may repeat ineffective behaviors.

This process of acquiring our communication skills has a lot to do with the common communication problems that we deal with daily. No two people have identical fields of experience. Even identical twins don't have the same field of experience because one was born first and the other second. The amount of shared understanding that occurs between two people depends on how much they have experienced that is in common. Most of us have some overlap of our fields of experience, called our area of shared understanding. Since our communication comes from our field of experience, it is natural that we have problems understanding each other. The area of shared understanding is probably fairly small when compared to the total of the many experiences that have shaped our communication.

Let me illustrate how our field of experience and area of shared understanding interact. The words we use are products of our field of experience. In my youth, when my family moved from Kentucky to Southeastern Ohio, I noticed that my new friends seemed to have an

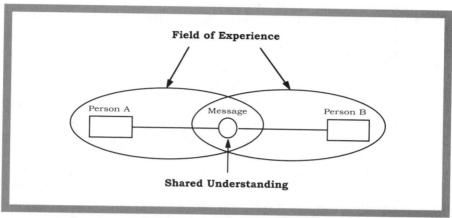

Field of Experience

Person A

Message

Person B

Shared Understanding

FIGURE 3-1. FIELD OF EXPERIENCE

unusual vocabulary. Things that were crooked or off-centered were called *whopperjawed*. When first introduced to this term, I replied, "Whopper what?" Once my friends explained the term, it was clear to me that they were describing a condition that I knew as *sighgoggling*. Don't run to your Funk & Wagnall's, because these words aren't in it. They are solely spoken words rather than written words. They are synonymous colloquial terms. How many of you in a whole year will use every word in the dictionary at least once? Nobody in the world does. We all use a set of words that are comfortable or common to us. Not everyone uses the same set of words, and each of us uses only a small subset of all the words in any dictionary, called an available pool of words. When we want to express a thought, we reach into this pool and select our words to send our message.

Another illustration of the impact of our field of experience on interpersonal understanding occurred when I was a sophomore in college. After my freshman year of college, I worked a year in the underground coal industry as a section ventilation man. Later, in my second year of college, my course work included a public speaking course. The requirements included making a presentation on any subject of interest to me. I decided to describe ventilation in the coal mine. I diligently prepared and organized my material. On the appointed day, I gave a speech using the terms inby, outby, returns, intakes, ribs, face, and other coal mine lingo. Had I been attentive, I might have noticed the vacant looks of the other students' faces and the professor scratching his head. As it turned out, I failed that speech. The failure did not reflect the validity of my presentation. If a group of coal miners had been in the audience, the content of my presentation would have been totally coherent. My failure was the result of poor audience analysis and the use of specialized terms used by coal miners that my audience was unfamiliar with.

What could I have done to connect with this audience and bring us both into the intersect of shared understanding? For one thing, it would have been useful to define all unique or unusual terms. A similar problem with term definition occurs when we talk about work with a neighbor or when we take a job with a new organization. Jargon communication is also apparent between departments in the same company. Be aware of how the person to whom you are speaking receives your message. Occasionally, question the other person as to the level of understanding. Another suggestion is to use more than one medium of communication. Pictures or drawings on a flip chart may help connect the field of experience. Also, illustrations of the principles that you are describing, using situations that are common to the person with whom you are communicating, would be useful. I could have illustrated the concept of ventilation in the underground mining industry with a simple comparison. I grew up in an old farm house with no air conditioning. In the summer we ventilated the house by opening two windows to create a draft. Mining ventilation used the same concept to ventilate a mining section. The avenue of the air course had to be open coming onto the section, across the section, and leaving the section. At the point where this air course was restricted or closed, the ventilation ceased. Finally, one of the best ways of connecting shared understanding between individuals is to physically go to the area you are describing and let the other person experience it personally.

Nonverbal Communication

What percentage of all the meaning that is transferred between two people is the result of verbal communication or nonverbal communication? Before you read further, write down the numbers that you believe describe the percentage that both verbal and nonverbal communication represent in shared understanding between two people. Later in this chapter I will share the results of research on this question.

When you think about it, we send a lot of nonverbal messages. Everything we do communicates something about us. According to experts, we develop our first impressions of each other within 15 seconds of meeting. How do we develop this rapid impression? We reach into our mental computers and pull out the most common experiences we have had. "He looks like my brother-in-law." "She sounds like my sister." We attach a similar judgment to the new person as we did to the past relationship. These impressions primarily arise from nonverbal cues. Some of the most important include: head nods, facial expressions, vocal expressions, gesturing, proxemics, body posture, touch, grooming, and pauses. Let's take a few minutes to expand on each of these different types of nonverbal messages.

Head nods can mean two very different things. On the one hand, a head nod may mean that I agree with the content of your message. On the other hand, I may be simply encouraging you to continue with your thoughts and comments in a nonverbal equivalent of, "I understand," or "I'm following you." As you can imagine, a misinterpretation of this nonverbal can create problems for both parties. If I interpret your head nod as agreement, and you meant it as understanding, we may walk away from the communication with very different feelings about our level of agreement.

Facial expressions are a major component of nonverbal communication. There is a continuum of expressions from the mindless smile to the deadpan look. Facial expressions are most effectively used to reflect changing emotions and messages. Eye contact is probably the single most important facial expression. Eye contact shows concern or attraction, builds relationships, and projects communication competence. Your eyes consistently reflect your thinking and feelings. Raised eyebrows reflect surprise. Wrinkles around the eyes show amusement. Few people can lie with their eyes. Eye contact demonstrates trustworthiness, confidence, and empathy.

Vocal expressions transmit a great deal of information by themselves. In some Far Eastern languages, up to twelve different meanings can be attached to the same word spoken in different tones. We can also tell a lot from vocal expressions in English. We make judgments about a person's sadness, excitement, interest, or disinterest just by the tone of the message. As a matter of fact, in phone communication, tone is the most important nonverbal cue we use.

Gesturing uses the hands as an added dimension to nonverbal communication. Many unique messages are in the domain of gestures. They range from the OK gesture made with the thumb and fore-finger to the outstretched middle finger. We all know exactly what is meant by these two gestures. Recently, an associate of mine lamented, "I wish I could learn to talk without using my hands." I explained that her use of her hands enhanced her message by adding a visual component to her verbal one. However, too much gesturing or gestures that are unnaturally out of sync with the message can be distracting. My daughter and I attended her college orientation lecture a few years ago. The administrator who was welcoming us to the college periodically stretched his arms out to his sides to make a point. This gesture was repeated several times in a short speech, but the gesture and his words were out of sync. My daughter finally leaned over to me and asked, "Dad, is he going to take off?" Even appropriate gestures can be distracting if not used effectively. An example of inappropriate gesturing occurred in a presentation that a colleague of mine attended. When I asked my peer what she had learned from the speaker, she replied, "Not a thing. He played with a rubber band the whole time, and I couldn't focus on anything else."

Proxemics is another component of nonverbal communication. It involves the personal space that we require and give to others and the movements that we make toward or away from one another. Status impacts the amount of space we give others. The higher the perceived status, the more space a person is given. Gender has been shown to be a determining factor in the amount of space given or demanded. Men automatically receive more space than women. This may in part be due to the differences in average size between men and women. Most people, however, attribute this occurrence to the sociological training that people receive. In our society, an arm's length of space is reserved for family and loved ones. Arm's length to five feet is the domain of the casual friend or acquaintance. Space beyond that distance belongs to the total stranger. There are also cultural dimensions to personal space. Southern Europeans, for example, command and give less personal space than people from some other cultures.

An engineer with whom I worked was a man of Greek background whose technical expertise was admired. However, a number of peers and plant workers complained that he "got in their faces" when talking to them. To the engineer, this behavior showed friendship, but his peers felt it impinged upon their private space. Several workers complained to me about the engineer, saying, "He gets so close to me, I think he's going to kiss me." I asked the engineer if he noticed that people often backed up when he tried to talk to them.

He had noticed, but didn't know what to make of it. I suggested that he take one step back from his communication comfort zone and see if people responded differently. He reported later that this simple technique made a great deal of difference in his ability to talk with others in the plant.

Proxemics also explains the uniqueness of elevator behavior. We are uncomfortable with having others forced into our personal space. If five people get on an elevator, the first one to board will probably take control of the buttons in the front corner. The second person will choose one of the remaining three corners. The third and fourth persons still have vacant corners from which to choose. Finally, the last person will be forced into the vulnerable center. In my training sessions, I use proxemics as an involvement tool with trainees (described in Chapter 7). If one person appears to be daydreaming or not involved with the session, I stand closer to him or her. This usually draws the trainee back into the session physically and intellectually. Equalizing the distance between individuals in a training program and myself helps the participants feel valued. Again, too much of this type of movement can be distracting. I remember a professor in a graduate course I took who incessantly paced back and forth in a Groucho Marx style of instruction. His content was important for me; however, his movements were hard to follow. By the middle of the semester, I had developed ping-pong neck.

Body posture is another component of nonverbal communication that projects confidence or lack of it to those around us. Slumped shoulders or straight posture are interpreted as a message of how you feel about yourself and your perception of your lot in life in general. Some questions arise regarding the interpretation of body posture and closure behavior. Most agree that crossed arms or crossed legs are often seen as an unconscious attempt to protect oneself. Attentive behavior includes having both feet squarely planted on the floor. Both hands are available for gesturing if they are resting on the arm of the chair or on your legs. Finally, a slight leaning forward shows concern and interest in what the other person is saying.

Touch is another very significant form of nonverbal communication. One of the most common methods of touch is the handshake, one of the many ways we say hello. Most agree that the handshake should be firm and confident, since weak or soft handshakes are interpreted as indicating lack of confidence or insecurity.

The initial eye contact and handshake together are largely responsible for the development of that first impression with a potential boss,

peer, or subordinate. Practice these behaviors and get critiques on yours. The ritual of handshaking varies among the cultures that practice it. A German man who began work in a West Virginia plant was insulted when after a couple of days the Americans didn't offer to shake hands with him anymore. In Germany, peers shake hands every day. In the United States, it is only an initial meeting behavior.

The demonstration of touch in our work society changed dramatically as a result of the Clarence Thomas—Anita Hill hearings. Who among us have not engaged in discussions about sexual harassment in recent years? We all feel differently about how much touch is appropriate in the workplace. Some of us tend to be back slappers and huggers, or what some people call touchers. Others of us are much less comfortable with any physical contact at work. How do you know if you are infringing upon another employee's comfort with touch? The individual may not be comfortable with telling you how he or she feels but will nonverbally indicate comfort or discomfort with your behavior. Be aware of the stiffening of a shoulder or movement away from a touch. The toucher may view this stiffening as a personal rejection. It is likely, however, that it is just a personal comfort factor for the nontoucher. The facilitative leader's obligation is to be aware of these messages and act in accordance with them.

Grooming and even our choices of clothing and jewelry are judgment messages that are sent and received by all of us. It is important to realize that your choices on these issues create impressions that others around you develop.

Pauses have significant nonverbal impact. Those who talk incessantly are often ineffective communicators. Pauses can improve their communication success. When we pause, others have an opportunity to think about our previous message and compose their thoughts about the subject at hand. Think about the occupations whose practitioners use pauses strategically. Effective attorneys, teachers, and comedians are a few that come to mind. Have you ever known a person who could not tell a joke? The problem is a poor sense of pause. Paul Harvey interjects strategically orchestrated pauses in his newscasts. His use of pauses creates interest in his listeners and is actually his signature as a radio and television personality.

Nonverbal symbols are not automatically culturally transferable. For example, in Asian cultures, head nodding is usually a gesture of respect rather than agreement. In Albania, head nodding means exactly the opposite of our interpretation. Side-to-side head nodding means yes, and up-and-down head nodding means no. Those who grew up in Asian cultures respond to eye contact very differently than Americans do. Eye contact early in the relationship may indicate lack of respect or status differentiation. Also in Asian cultures our handshake is replaced with a bow. Hand gestures that are appropriate and common in our culture can really get you in trouble in other countries. Other nonverbals that have various sexual connotations are the thumb and forefinger making a circle in Brazil, Germany, and Turkey; fingers crossed in Paraguay; finger snaps with both hands in France and Belgium; tapping index fingers in Egypt; a fist slap in Italy and Chile; a forearm jerk in Mediterranean countries; thumbs up in Australia; the palms pressed together with fingers spread in Nigeria; and the thumb extending between the index and middle finger in some European and Mediterranean countries (Axtell, 1993). A Turkish supervisor and his staff expressed surprise in a training session because of the culturally different interpretation of the thumb and forefinger gesture. In our society, it means that everything's good, or okay. In Turkey, it is a nonverbal way of calling someone a homosexual. These two different meanings could get someone in trouble. There are many other examples of nonverbals that mean different things depending upon the cultural definition. As our workforce becomes more culturally diverse, it is important to be aware of these potential areas of misunderstanding.

Most important, nonverbals must be congruent with the conversation in which you are involved. Lack of congruence between your verbal and nonverbal messages creates mistrust on the part of the receiver of your communication. We always believe the nonverbal message when it conflicts with the verbal message. How should you interpret the message of a person who is smiling broadly while describing how sad he or she is? The reason we believe the nonverbal message over the verbal message is that we learned nonverbal communication first. Our first language is nonverbal; English is our second language. Young babies identify nonverbally whether their parents are happy or sad. When a parent looks over the crib's edge and smiles at a baby, the baby reacts instinctively. When a parent is sick or sad and looks over the crib, the baby often starts crying. If you observe babies, you will notice that they mimic the emotions of the adults and other children around them.

Now, let's refer back to my earlier question. What percentage of our meaning is transferred by verbal messages and what percentage is attributed to nonverbal messages? Has your judgment of the impact of nonverbal communication changed? Harrison (1970) suggests that 65 percent of the meaning communicated between individuals is nonverbal in nature. Other researchers suggest that over 90 percent of our message contents are sent and received through nonverbal channels (McCroskey & Wheeless, 1976).

Listening

The single most important communication skill that organizational members need to develop and facilitative leaders need to demonstrate is listening. Listening involves a set of verbal and nonverbal skills. All of the communication skills are rooted in listening ability. The single biggest complaint that subordinates make about their supervisors is, "They don't listen to us."

What is listening? How does it differ from hearing? Some people use the terms interchangeably, but they are different activities. Listening is a selective process. One purposefully demonstrates certain behaviors when listening. Hearing, however, is a physiological process. Hearing is the sensory processing of stimuli that constantly bombard your ears. We hear 24 hours a day. However, we disregard the great majority of the data. Listening is a subset of hearing.

Take a minute and lay down this book. On a sheet of paper, write down all the sounds you hear. How many did you list—the fluorescent

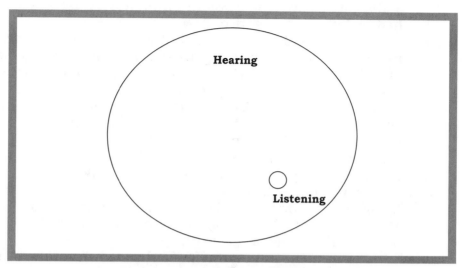

FIGURE 3-2. RELATIONSHIP OF LISTENING TO HEARING

lights buzzing; a car going by outside; a baby crying; someone laughing in the next room? While you were reading the beginning of this chapter you heard a number of the same sounds that you just listed. However, when you put down the book and concentrated, you began to listen. Listening is paying attention to or attending to the stimuli or people around you.

We pay attention to one another verbally and nonverbally. Nonverbally, when people are listening to me, I see them nod their heads, look at me, face forward in my direction, and exhibit facial expressions of raised eyebrows and wrinkles of concentration. If people demonstrate these behaviors, we tend to believe that they are listening to us.

Years ago when I was teaching an undergraduate course at Ohio University, one student demonstrated many nonverbal listening behaviors. I made a judgment that he was focusing on the material I was presenting. However, he didn't offer responses to my questions in class, and I didn't call on him specifically. One day, I posed a question for the students and asked them to jot down their thoughts. I walked around the room to see if they were able to answer the question and if they were finished. What do you think I saw on this student's paper? Oodles of doodles. Not one pearl of wisdom that had fallen out of my mouth landed on his page. The student had learned to fake listening and create positive impressions on professors. He was a senior, so he had had plenty of practice.

Verbal listening is also demonstrated by identifiable behaviors. The verbal behaviors can be categorized as neutral encouragement, restatement, reflection, clarifying, paraphrasing, summary statements, and open-ended questions. Neutral encouragement is almost in between verbal and nonverbal listening. The listener may say things like, "I see. Uh-huh. That's interesting. I understand." The listener isn't adding content to the other person's message but is merely showing attention. Someone who is demonstrating neutral encouragement is trying to give the floor to the other person. Some of my clients have expressed the idea that a similar set of behaviors could be interpreted as a dismissal. If you really don't care about what the other person is saying, an attempt at neutral encouragement may be taken as lack of interest because of the tone of the voice.

Restatement is repeating the last statement of the other party, as in, "You feel this evaluation is unfair." When this statement is followed by silence, the other party is prompted to clarify the statement and give additional information.

Reflection refers to statements that describe what you see the other person doing physically; for example, "As you mentioned Joan's name, you frowned." A reflecting statement usually prompts an explanation of how the other person feels. Let me describe a conversation with a manager who was a peer of mine. He and I were becoming increasingly angry with each other. When I realized the escalation of emotion, I first disclosed my own feelings by describing the tightness in my chest as my stress level was building. Then I described the redness in his face and the increasing volume of both of our voices. These statements did not evaluate the merit of our positions in the argument. I stated facts, not opinions. The statements did raise our awareness of the emotional level of the conversation. Both of us proceeded to take control of ourselves and reduced the tension. We agreed to continue the discussion at another time and so avoid saying things that might have had a lasting negative effect on our relationship. The situation was dealt with to both our satisfaction at the next meeting, after we had both had time to cool off.

Clarifying questions assist the listener in exploring different sides of a problem. Examples are, "Where did you first see this problem demonstrated?" or, "Is this occurring on all three shifts?" These questions help narrow the discussion to specifics.

Paraphrasing is a technique of rephrasing the other party's thoughts in your own words.

Statement: "Glenn, we are not going to be able to complete this job in the agreed time frame."

Paraphrase: "So, you believe the time frame is too short?"

Clarification: "No, I think we need to work some overtime in order to complete the project on time."

The purpose of this technique is to validate your understanding of what the other person is saying or to correct it in part or in whole. Often we assume that we have a shared understanding of the topic being discussed. Later, we realize that we were talking about two very different things. Paraphrasing is probably the most prevalently used verbal listening behavior. When you add paraphrasing to the nonverbal listening behaviors, it is virtually impossible to fake listening.

Summary statements include several paraphrases that end in a directional suggestion for the group. They are very useful in business meetings, when discussions appear to be nonproductive or circular in nature; for example, "So, you think we need to address this quality problem, address it by next week, and involve Joe, Sally, and the customer. Let's get everyone together and plan our approach." Summary statements can be employed to bring a meeting back on track or as a transition to another set of discussions. At the conclusions of meetings, these statements are also very valuable. They identify the agreements and disagreements of the meeting and list the actions to be taken.

Finally, open-ended questions are extremely useful listening tools. Open-ended questions result in less prescribed responses. Closed-ended questions prescribe short answers such as yes, no, or maybe. An example of an open-ended question is, "How do you feel about this approach?" An example of a closed-ended question is, "Do you like this approach?" Open-ended questions demonstrate respect for the thoughts and feelings of the other person more than closed-ended questions do. However, open-ended questions also require more time than closed-ended questions.

I first became aware of listening as a set of behaviors while pursuing my master's degree. After a description and demonstration of listening behaviors by the professor, the class was broken into dyads. Each pair of students took turns describing a recent nonthreatening event in their lives and practicing the different listening behaviors. When I went home that night, I continued my practice. Instead of reading the paper and responding to my wife's review of her day's events with grunts, I put down the paper, looked at her, and practiced the listening behaviors. At first, she gave me a puzzled look. Then she asked me if I felt all right. Finally, she asked me what I was doing. Her communication was more in-depth and animated. Later, as we were discussing the skill of listening, she confessed that she felt very good about my new behavior.

I continued my practice at work where I was a foreman for a track construction crew. I found that my new listening skills encouraged a flood of communication from some members of my crew. I realized that I had to be strategic with my use of listening behaviors. Many people are starved for this type of attention. I decided to select my listening events and to devote total attention to the other person when I was listening. I would choose a place where we could be alone and uninterrupted, even taking the phone off the hook. I made sure that each member of the team had an opportunity to be heard.

Each of the verbal listening behaviors demonstrates that you are paying attention to the other person. You will not be able to perform the verbal listening behaviors if you are not listening and attending to the other person.

In order to increase the level of shared understanding, first take responsibility for more than just sending a communication. Observe the other person's nonverbal reaction to your message. Give the same message in more than one way. Ask questions about the other person's understanding. Take time to pay attention and listen to the other person. Define any unusual words and terms. Check the validity of your interpretation of nonverbal signals with the person demonstrating them. Only he or she truly knows what is meant by a particular nonverbal cue.

Interpersonal communication involves a complex set of behaviors. Since most of the work accomplished in organizations is realized through communication, the facilitative leader needs to be aware of the dynamics of communication and demonstrate a proactive attitude toward improving communication skills.

Summary

This chapter focused on the communication behaviors of the facilitative leader. Chapter contents covered why we communicate the way we do, how our fields of experience are developed, and the extent to which they overlap with areas of shared understanding. The uniqueness of our nonverbal communication and its impact on shared understanding between people was explored. Finally, the verbal and nonverbal behaviors that combine to make up what we call facilitative listening were described in detail.

Questions from Chapter 3

1. Think about the last time you were misunderstood or misunderstood someone else. What could you have done differently to create more shared understanding?
   A. As the sender?
   B. As the receiver?
2. Why are nonverbals the greater part of our communication messages?
3. Why do we believe nonverbal messages even when they are in conflict with verbal messages?
4. Identify at least four nonverbal listening behaviors.
5. Identify the seven verbal listening behaviors.

Actions from Chapter 3

1. Make a list of jargon terms or acronyms that you use regularly. Remember to make an effort to define these terms when talking to someone outside of your field.
2. Sit with a friend in a restaurant or library and jot down all the different types of nonverbal behaviors you observe. Then write down the meaning you attributed to each nonverbal. Compare the two lists for commonalities and differences.
3. Choose two listening behaviors that you don't presently use and practice them with a friend.
4. Choose a friend or family member with whom you spend time. Ask this person for feedback on the nonverbal behaviors you demonstrate when you get upset. Note these behaviors in chronological sequence and try to increase your awareness of when you demonstrate the early stages of emotion. This awareness will help you make behavioral decisions that can de-escalate your emotion.

Developer of People

Definition

The third mode of the facilitative leader is that of a developer of people and teams. This chapter focuses on the developer of people. The facilitative leader models effective and respectful communication skills and doesn't hesitate to teach these skills to anyone who is willing to learn them. The leader demonstrates new skills and gives feedback to others in the workplace who attempt to practice these skills. The feedback must be clear, descriptive, and not personally evaluative. It is important that the feedback message express your feelings in a nonemotional manner. If the message concerns a problem, focus on constructive behaviors for the future rather than on blaming statements about the past. Finally, explain the consequences if the desired events occur or do not occur. This feedback technique is described more fully in Chapter 6.

I once heard a humorous story that is the antithesis of my prescription for how to develop people but is not that far from some of my experiences in the coal mine. It seems a man was walking uneventfully to an appointment when he caught up with a blind gentleman and his seeing eye dog walking in the same direction just as all three of them stopped for a red light. The first man was watching the dog when the animal hiked its leg and soaked the blind man from the leg down. Amazed at this turn of events, the first man decided to keep his mouth shut to avoid further embarrassment to the blind gentleman. At that moment, the blind gentleman reached into his pocket, pulled out a dog biscuit, and held it down to his dog. At this point the first man had to break his silence. He turned to the blind man and said, "Mister, I just have to tell you, after what that dog did to you, that was the kindest thing I've ever seen anyone do." The blind man wrinkled up his face in puzzlement and said, "Kind! I'm just trying to find out where his head is so I can kick his ass." This type of development process is attempted daily in many of our organizations, where employees are threatened, shamed, and blamed into new behaviors.

The Learner

A focus on learning is very critical to the facilitative leader. This learning focus concerns both the facilitative leader and other organizational members. The learner element of the facilitative leader implies a sensitivity to the needs, values, and experience of others. The facilitative leader understands that the learning organization requires a cadre of learning individuals (Senge, 1990). The facilitative leader looks at experiences and relationships as opportunities to gain additional skills and insights. Learning from others requires that one respect the needs, abilities, and knowledge of others. Block (1981) suggests that respect is demonstrated and gained by encouraging dialogue with others even though you may disagree with their positions. The facilitative leader must demonstrate respect of a variety of opinions in order to create a consensus for action. Learning from one another shows that respect.

Adults come to a learning experience with general characteristics that have implications for teaching and everyday interactions. The fact is that adults are different from younger people. Developers of adults should be aware of these differences and characteristics. Knowles (1980) proposes a movement from pedagogy to andragogy. However, in both processes, the leader has the responsibility to encourage and nurture the learner. Pedagogy places the responsibility for learning on the leader. The learner is dependent on the leader for definition of what needs to be learned, how it is to be learned, and evaluation of whether or not it has been learned. Other pedagogical principles suggest that the learner's experience is insignificant in the learning process; all learners are at the same starting point for standardized, uniform training. Awareness of application of the learning is not necessary during the learning; it will be apparent later. Andragogy is a process whereby the learner is more self-directed and takes responsibility for the learning. It consists of a number of opposing principles, described here.

First, adults have had many life experiences. In order to capitalize on these experiences, leaders should get to know other organizational members and learn about their past experiences. I have found in working with a variety of diverse groups that there is something I can learn from everyone, if I take the time to listen to them. When in dialogue with others, try to relate your illustrations or points to their experiences. Encourage others to use their experiences in accomplishing learning tasks. Allow them flexibility in designing their learning processes. Use others as resource persons. Some of the most motivating experiences I have had occurred when someone asked me to teach him or her something. I felt valued by the request. Help others to recognize and respect one another's experience. Celebrate the successes of individuals on your team and refer others to individuals with special knowledge. This process can create an interdependent learning team.

Second, adults are highly motivated to learn. Remember, the desire on the part of most adults is to make direct use of the knowledge they have gained. Therefore, organizational meetings (and training sessions) should provide the learners with usable knowledge that can be applied immediately to everyday work life as well as to life outside work. Although most of the training I perform is focused on work related issues, often participants share with me that they realized the greatest utilization of the material at home.

At the end of each training session I facilitate key learnings and action planning exercises described later in the chapter. These exercises highlight the critical learnings of the session and focus participants on immediate use of the skills and information shared in the session.

Adults have many different roles and responsibilities with competing demands upon their time. One of my greatest fears as a trainer is to waste people's time in a session. We are judged harshly when we waste people's time. Given that adults are highly motivated to learn, there are several techniques for enabling their learning. Identify the concerns and goals of others and relate them to the task at hand. Encourage others to be involved in the planning of learning goals and activities to match their roles and responsibilities. An expectations check described in Chapter 5 allows participants to state their specific needs from the learning event. Select materials and approaches that are oriented to adult roles. Recognize that if the needs of the person with whom you are communicating are not being met, other responsibilities will take higher priority. They will mentally take a trip and fail to focus on your communication. If individuals are involved in identifying and planning their learning goals, they value the process and are more likely to stay focused and less likely to feel the session is a waste of time.

Third, some adults lack confidence in their ability to learn. Many of us have separated our lives into the learning part and the doing part. We look at learning as the formal school portion of our lives. Once we complete that part, then the rest of our lives are dedicated to doing more important things in the "real world." Discuss this commonly held fear with employees early in the development process to alleviate their concerns. During my college experience, there were several times when I stayed out of the classroom for a year or more. When I returned, I felt some stress about my capability to be successful in that learning environment. To alleviate self-doubt, design short-term learning goals with your staff so that each individual has an opportunity for success, early and frequently. Cut the material to be learned into manageable pieces. Don't overwhelm the learner. The learning experience must be satisfying, and your team member should feel a sense of accomplishment at frequent points. People tend to persist in a task, no matter how difficult, if they are getting enough satisfaction from it.

Fourth, adults vary more from each other than young people do. Develop individualized means for meeting individual needs, when possible, in terms of goals and approaches to meeting goals. Encourage team members to recognize and accept individual differences among themselves and others. Use these differences, which represent strengths, by having team members share their experiences and serve as resource persons for the rest of the group. There is increasing evidence that diverse work teams are more effective, resulting in higher-quality decisions and products (Fernandez, 1993). Work team diversity enables people to look at problems with a fresh set of eyes and new approaches.

How Adults Learn Best

Knowles (1980) describes several techniques for enhancing learning among adults. I describe five: actively involve team members, set an appropriate climate, focus learning on problem solving, let team members set the pace, and give feedback about progress. First, active participation by team members is important in setting goals for learning. Identify why a particular area of learning is important to the team and to the organization. The WIIFO-WIIFM exercise described in Chapter 2 is a useful tool for discussing the whys behind any initiative. Encourage team members to work with you in formulating objectives. Goals that you or others develop and hand to a team will remain your goals and might not be adopted by the team members. Consider using group discussions to actively involve your trainees in formulating learning objectives (see the Goal Setting section in Chapter 5).

Second, learning should take place in an appropriate climate that includes both physical and emotional elements. Build an educative environment that is respectful of all team members by encouraging decision making by team members, freely sharing information, stressing mutual responsibility in setting learning goals, designing comfortable facilities, being informal, and answering questions fully. Team member participation in decision making creates ownership to implement the solution. If the decision impacts the team and team members have the required information, they should be given the right to make the decision. Promote freedom and availability of information. The general rule should be to share any information that a team needs or wants unless there is a clear business need that prevents you from doing so. This approach is the opposite of the "need to know" approach. Stress mutual responsibility in defining goals for learning. Physical conditions should be comfortable and appropriate for adults. Too many organizations skimp on meeting room facilities. Chairs are hard and ventilation is inadequate. People spend a great deal of time in these rooms addressing value-added issues for the organization. Let me suggest that when bodies are tired, for all practical purposes the meeting is over. Informality should be encouraged between the leader and team members. Always answer questions fully and carefully, remembering that there are many levels of ability and background among adults. Allow trainees the choices of when to get a cup of coffee or make a comment.

Third, learning should be problem-centered. The facilitative leader focuses on problem solving rather than on blaming. The objective is learning, not identifying the culprit. When you enter into dialogue with team members, make sure that the issue is defined and clarified and the objective is stated. Once a problem is identified, many organizations focus on who made the mistake rather than inventing actions that will prevent reoccurences. Blaming is a waste of time. It seldom solves the problem and always lowers the self-esteem of an employee or team.

Fourth, adults learn most effectively when they set their own pace. Allow team members to proceed at their own rate, because we all learn at different rates and through different mediums. Differences in learning styles are not a function of intelligence. One relative of mine is an auditory learner. I, however, am a visual learner. At times when watching television, I will remark that an actor was also featured in another television show a few years ago. She often argues with me as to the identification of the actor. Several times we have waited for the credits to settle the disagreement. On the other hand, she is often able to identify an actor from another room, simply by voice. Her learning style is different from mine but just as accurate.

Finally, the trainee should receive feedback about progress toward goals. Use self-assessment forms that enable the trainees to keep track of their own progress. Encourage the trainees to clarify their goals and use them to review their progress.

Learning Techniques

One way to gain respect is to request feedback from other organizational members and act upon the information gained. Self-assessment techniques are also critical tools that the continual learner uses. Examples of assessment techniques include 360-degree feedback, which involves having feedback questionnaires completed by peers, subordinates, and the supervisor. The feedback is then given to the target person by a third party. There are several 360-degree surveys available in the marketplace. Copies of the survey are distributed to subordinates, peers, and supervisors selected by the target person. The target person also completes the survey. All responses are returned to a consultant for compilation and analysis. Finally, the target person receives feedback from a psychologist or trained feedback giver. Action plans are developed for the target person based upon the data compiled.

Another learning technique, called expectations communication, involves face-to-face feedback forums with the whole team. The structure of the forum and the items to be discussed are determined and communicated prior to the session. Each participant then prepares his or her thoughts on the agenda items.

It is critical that individuals in groups understand what is required of them by all other group members, especially the leader. The expectations communication process is designed to identify and elaborate on the expectations and needs of all members of a work team. Usually, this process is initiated by the leader. However, it can be suggested by any member of the work group. In essence, the outcome of this process is role clarification, whereby each team member has a turn to describe the value that he or she contributes to the team. The following are sample questions:

What experiences of mine are useful?

What are the most important functions that I perform?

What am I willing to do for this team?

Each team member then describes his or her specific expectations and needs of other team members in terms of resources, information, or cooperation. Each expectation should be prefaced with continue, start, or stop.

It may be important to have a neutral facilitator lead this session. With a neutral facilitator, the facilitative leader can participate more completely in the session. During the meeting, the facilitative leader can list the action items that are identified and observe the dynamics of the group interaction. The key points should be reviewed at the end of the session.

Finally, the group prioritizes the points and develops action plans to implement them effectively. Individual responsibilities, timelines, and accountabilities are clarified. I developed this technique based upon Looram's (1985) work on the transition meeting with new supervisors and workers. When I was the plant training manager at BorgWarner Chemicals, several supervisors made the comment that they had to train a new building manager, again. Upon further investigation I found that the issue was that some particular managers' jobs were used as tests for young, fast-track employees. Unfortunately, the frequent changes placed a burden on the supervisors and workers who had to learn all over how to interact successfully with a new manager. Sometimes it took several months for the parties to be comfortable with one another. During this period of uncertainty, aggressive business decisions were postponed which negatively impacted the group's outcomes. The expectations communication technique was useful as a jump start for these new relationships. The technique has also proven to be useful as a final activity in a weeklong team-building program.

Interpersonal feedback, a third learning technique, involves a neutral party who designs an interview guide to gather information about the target person, who will then receive the feedback. Common questions include:

1. How do you feel about Pat as a supervisor (peer, subordinate)?
2. Describe Pat's communication and interaction style.
3. Can you tell me some stories about things that have happened to Pat?
4. What does Pat do that is very effective?
5. On what communication or relationship issues does Pat need to work?
6. Describe Pat's listening skills.
7. How does Pat react when he or she is happy with you? When he or she is angry with you?
8. How effectively does Pat motivate others?
9. Describe Pat's delegation skills.
10. How does Pat deal with conflict?
11. Does Pat give you the information you need to do your job?
12. Does Pat give you the feedback on your performance that you need?
13. Would you like to have more or less interaction with Pat?
14. Do you trust Pat?
15. Is Pat a trusting person?
16. Is Pat sincere?
17. What one thing could Pat do that would most improve the morale and productivity of this group?
18. What else can you tell me that Pat should know?

Once the interview guide is completed, an internal person other than the target person is selected. This internal person sets up interviews with 7 to 10 employees who work around Pat and have an opportunity to observe his or her behaviors. The target person generally doesn't know the identity of the interviewees. Next, the neutral party conducts the interviews. Note taking is preferred over tape recording, as the data collection process impacts the openness of the interviewees. Once the data are gathered, a summary is typed. Then, an analysis is performed on the data using a highlight reduction process. Items that are frequently mentioned or described with intensity are selected and marked with a highlighter pen. All other verbiage is eliminated. Then the highlight process is repeated a second time to identify two lists. The first list, containing comments regarding the target person's strengths, is presented and discussed. The second list consists of items that the target person should work on improving. The target person has a week to consider the items he or she would be willing and able to work on, then chooses only two items and meets with the neutral party to do action planning. Periodic feedback sessions are held by phone to discuss the development progress of the target person.

Feedback for Joe Smith
August 20, 1998

Strengths
Management Skills

1. Taught me budgets.
2. Very knowledgeable about our jobs.
3. Knows laws and regulations that apply to his department.
4. Helped us get needed departmental improvements.
5. Great organizer.
6. Good administratively.
7. Can handle multiple tasks and functions.
8. Good numbers guy.
9. Gives us challenging tasks.

Interpersonal Skills

1. Has improved in the past six months.

Feedback for Joe Smith
August 20, 1998

Development Areas
Interpersonal Communication

1. Confuses people by providing too much information and detail. Key points get lost. He goes on tangents.
2. Doesn't give you time to ask questions.
3. When he disagrees with someone, he sometimes says, "Wrong answer."
4. Gets mad when questioned.

5. Uncomfortable with small talk in person or on the phone.
6. Doesn't consult peers before his decisions.
7. Perceived as opinionated and arrogant.

Listening

1. Needs to listen more and talk less.
2. Has an answer immediately.
3. Only hears pieces he wants to.

Management Skills

1. Gives authoritative directives.
2. Takes credit for other people's ideas.
3. He tells you every step. Makes you feel like you don't know anything.
4. Doesn't ask questions or communicate whys.
5. Hands out accountability but not responsibility.
6. Communication meetings too long and unnecessary.
7. Takes time to decipher handwriting.
8. Anything we write we have to redo 3–4 times.

A similar process that I call a culture check is designed to learn about the culture of the entire organization. I interview a representative cross section of the organization. Then I perform the highlight reduction process described above. The results are useful data for organizational decisions and to focus organizational learning. Training and development efforts are often planned using this data. Some culture check questions are as follows:

1. How would you describe the communication that you experience here?
2. Do you feel that others listen to you?
3. Do you get the information that you need to do your job?
4. Do you get the feedback on your performance that you need?
5. How well are resources utilized here?
6. How do people deal with conflict here?
7. Could you describe the trust level here?
8. What one thing would most improve the morale and productivity of this group?
9. What else can you tell me that I should know?

A fourth technique, called key learnings, is a process whereby I ask leaders to take a few minutes regularly to document the key learnings they have experienced. This exercise helps in two ways. First, the leader becomes more aware of the changes and learnings with which he or she is dealing daily. Second, the documentation of key learnings helps leaders organize their thoughts in order to transfer these learnings to other organization members. These key learnings were identified at the end of the second day of a three-day team-building session:

- Review the keys of listening.
- Practice listening.
- Be more attentive to my nonverbals and to those of others.
- Ask questions about my assumptions on the nonverbals of others.
- Identify the value of open-ended questions.
- Check with the other person as to their understanding of my nonverbals.
- Summarize statements of other participants.

I use the time I spend driving home from work each day to identify my key learnings of the day. This processing of the day's events helps me focus on improvements for the next day. A couple of years ago, my daughter and I took a walk in the woods. As we returned, I nonchalantly asked her if she could identify two key learnings that she had gained during the hike. She thought for a moment, somewhat surprised by the question, and then responded. "Well, I never knew before that the spicebush is the sole food source of the spicebush swallowtail butterfly and that if spicebush plants became extinct so would the spicebush butterfly. I also never heard the term embrication, which is a word that describes the way floods place flat rocks like a set of toppled dominoes oriented downstream." Key learnings are not just work related or school related. They happen in every part of our lives.

My first day at work in the coal mine was a significant learning experience for me. Actually, it was a shocking experience, rich with key learnings, but a poor example of effective people development (Ray, 1993). When I arrived at the mine for my first day's work, the shift foreman gave me a short lecture on how to use a self-rescuer and a couple of signals with my caplight. Then he introduced me to my foreman and walked away. The elevator doors opened, my boss walked on, and I followed. In a matter of seconds the doors opened again and I was a coal miner. In short, I learned by trial and error. Some of the miners gave me tips here and there, but I was largely on my own. This type of training is still prevalent in many industries. Some people call it puppy dog training. You put the new employee with an experienced employee, and the new employee follows around the experienced employee like a puppy dog and hopes the skills rub off. This development process for new employees in the coal mines changed a few months after I started when a new miner was killed in a machine accident. The key learnings from my orientation to coal mining were that concentration can enable one to be successful in new situations, and that with determination we can accomplish many things that we believed were impossible. (After the Bhopal disaster in which over 2,000 people died, the chemical industry also saw the importance of more effective training for new employees.) At BorgWarner Chemical while I was the training manager, we went from puppy dog training to a twelve-day orientation program for new employees.

One startup organization I work with has discussed the implementation of a learning bonus for employees. The organization will decide upon an appropriate number of hours for the bonus. Hours will be earned when employees attend seminars, take college classes (whether for credit or not), attend a professional conference, participate in a discussion group with other employees, join a book-of-the-month club, spend time mentoring another employee, conduct research, write articles or books, rent educational videos, or take advantage of other innovative opportunities for learning. Any employee who documents earning the required number of learning hours will receive a financial bonus. How does this benefit the organization? The obvious desired outcome is gaining needed skills, but it also creates renewal or reignition of excitement about the job.

The Tortoise Paradigm Revisited

We all remember hearing the fable of the tortoise and the hare. The rabbit represented speed and agility. The tortoise represented consistent, dogged progress. In the 1990s, organizations are following the rabbit's path and ignoring the value of the tortoise. External environmental factors have driven organizations in the hare's direction. International competition and globalization prominently impact the

DRAWING BY AUDREY TATUM

choices of organizational leaders. In some ways, the focus on speed at all costs is sacrificing organizational members and the organization's future ability to be successful. By the late 1980s, leading U.S. companies began wholesale trimming of employees at all levels. The stock market rewarded each downsizing effort with skyrocketing stock prices. Other companies watched the results of these leaders and were coerced by the stock market to act in accordance. Like dominoes, companies followed suit. In the past, it was true that organizations in this country, as well as elsewhere, were fatter than necessary. However, an unintended and largely ignored result of downsizing or rightsizing has been a dramatic erosion of the loyalty of all employees, from the president to the worker on the floor. This organizational direction needs to be turned around. We need to capitalize on the strength of diverse Americans and enable them once again to choose to commit themselves to their organizations.

There are several important constituencies within organizations, including customers, employees, stockholders, and management. Each of these groups is due a portion of the success of the organization. The customers are primary, for without them there is no reason for the organization to exist. All organizational members should focus on meeting customers' needs. The employees are also vital to the organization's success and should be considered critical to the accomplishment of the organization's goals. Employees should be treated as partners to the organization's purpose and should share in the organization's outcomes. Stockholders, who invest the money that allows the organization to meet its commitments and opportunities, must be rewarded in a way that encourages them to continue investing. The management of the organization has an investment in the organization's success as well. They need to set up structures and systems both to enable the success of employees and to meet customer needs. If managers do not perform this function, they are not needed. Successful organizations are designed to create positive outcomes for all of these different constituencies. The order of importance in the 1990s seems to have been perverted to the following order: stockholder, customer, management, and then employees. One of the purposes of this book is to reorder the priority of constituents to: customer, employee, management, and then stockholder. If the other constituencies' needs are met, the stockholders' financial needs will be met. To meet the customer's needs, employees must be enabled to feel confident and committed to the organization and to feel that the organization is committed to them. Dedicating resources to develop employees is one way that the organization can show commitment to them.

One day while canoeing on the Little Hocking River, I was paddling upstream. It had rained all night, and the river was bank full. My objective on this trip was to relax and observe nature. As I quietly proceeded upstream, I watched what I thought was a leaf being blown across the surface of the water. As I got closer, I could see the ripple of foot action in the water and the unmistakable orange and black head of a tortoise poking out of the water. At first, I thought, "Isn't it out of its element? Don't tortoises live exclusively on land?" Never had I seen one in the middle of the river.

About this time, the tortoise saw me and ducked its head under the water with the top of its shell floating. The evasive action didn't last long, and the tortoise came up for a gulp of air, paddling frantically. Finally, it approached the opposite bank and climbed out.

A lot of organizational members today feel like a land turtle in the water. They are asked to do things that take them out of their element and for which they were not trained. When washed into the river, the tortoise instinctively began swimming. However, our instincts in organizations are not as fine-tuned. When danger comes around the corner, employees duck for cover, knowing the cover can only be temporary. At other times employees become defensive, a counterproductive set of behaviors in any organization. Finally, as they always knew they had to, employees do the job as best they can to meet the organization's goals. It is the facilitative leader's obligation to assess organizational members and provide development opportunities to survive the leap into uncharted waters.

Employee Development

One very important function of the facilitative leader is to construct ongoing personal development plans and to encourage and lead other group members to develop their own plans. Five- to ten-year plans are appropriate for this activity, known as personal visioning or career development. The process involves reviewing your skill set and identifying future desired activities. A good question to begin this process is, "What would you like to be doing five years from now?" Once you identify that role, explore what skills will be needed to accomplish the new role. The facilitative leader administers this same process with his or her staff. Spend time frequently with other organizational members to discuss their progress on personal goals.

As you expend resources on the development of any employee or group of employees, a three-step development flow is important. See Figure 4-1.

First, talk with the individual or group about the learning objectives of the development initiative. What do you expect this activity to do for the business? Second, provide dedicated time for the employee to attend and focus on the development activity. Have the business pay the expenses for this learning opportunity. Make sure that someone else at work is meeting the business responsibilities of the employee being developed so that his or her complete attention can be on learning and internalizing skills. Third, hold a postdevelopment discussion with the learner. This is important for several reasons. You need to know if the business objectives have been met because you will be expecting the employee to be able to perform the desired behaviors. You also need to know if you should develop other employees in a similar manner or choose new development mechanisms. I revisited a plant where I had performed a daylong training program on communication. I asked one of the trainees how he felt about the training once he returned to work. He responded, "Not one supervisor or manager asked me if I liked the training, learned anything in the training, or thought it was worthwhile." To this individual, the lack of communication after the training meant that it wasn't too important

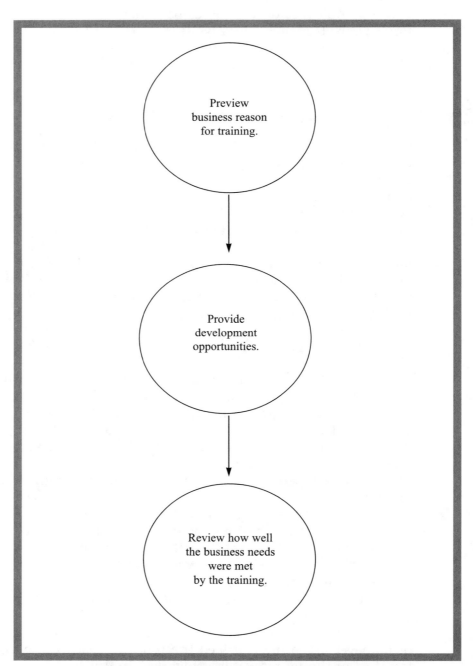

FIGURE 4-1. CAPITALIZING ON DEVELOPMENT ACTIVITIES

communication after the training meant that it wasn't too important to the management of the plant.

Another development process that is very important to employees and organizations is performance appraisal. Although the appraisal process is not viewed in a positive light by many employees, they do have a desire to understand how others value their performance. The problem with performance appraisals is that too often they are done poorly. Some supervisors are too lenient, giving everyone high ratings whether they deserve them or not. This performance appraisal error is called the halo effect. The halo effect demoralizes those who work hard and receive the same rating as those who don't care. There is nothing wrong with all employees getting high ratings if their performance warrants the rating. Some organizations use a forced ranking mechanism which guarantees that every employee gets a unique numerical rating. The objective behind this process is to thwart the halo effect. Unfortunately, the results are not an accurate reflection of the performance of the employees. As a matter of fact, if an organization is selecting employees that fit the tasks required by the organization and giving constructive feedback, you would expect more employees on the positive end of the scale. The thinking behind this method of appraisal is that there should be employees at all rating levels. Other supervisors err in the direction of strictness. They believe that lower ratings will encourage stronger efforts and continual performance improvements. But the opposite usually occurs, as employees become frustrated and view the system as irrelevant. Another performance appraisal error, called central tendency, is demonstrated by the supervisor who refuses to make discriminatory judgments and gives everyone the same middle-of-the-road rating. Again, this approach makes the performance appraisal process a nonevent.

Another problem with performance appraisal arises when the form used is outdated and does not reflect the critically desired behaviors for today. Many organizations hire performance appraisal experts to modify their forms and processes. Perhaps a better way to improve the performance appraisal system is to use the ideas of the employees themselves. I've been involved with two organizations that used this cross-functional approach (Ray, et al., 1997). First we assembled a group that represented all segments and levels of the organization. After some initial team-building, we began brainstorming the behaviors that would make the organization successful in five years. The discussions were lively and productive, and we agreed upon seven categories. Then the group began benchmarking performance appraisal forms and processes of var-

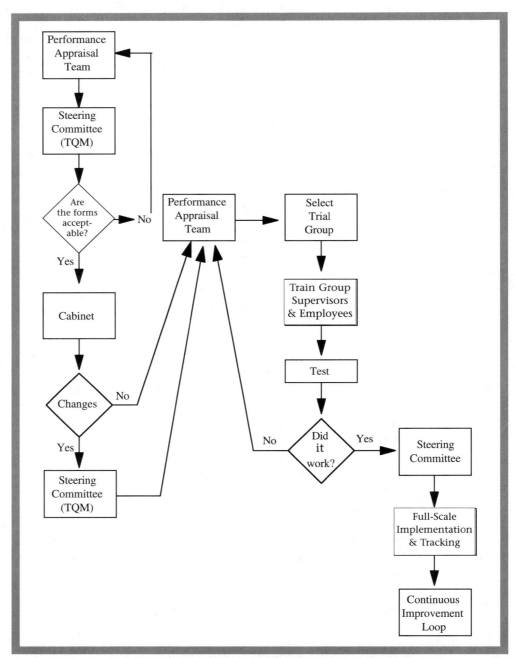

FIGURE 4-2. PERFORMANCE APPRAISAL DEVELOPMENT

ious other organizations. The process took quite a while but resulted in more buy-in than a top-down, mandated process would.

Summary

Chapter 4 elaborated on the mode of the facilitative leader as a developer of people. The focus on learning and the andragogy of adult learning theory in particular were described. Techniques for enabling learning in organizations were explored. Also, a three-step organizational process for developing employees, involving training preview, administration, and review, was explained. Finally, the importance of effective performance appraisal for employee development was emphasized.

Questions from Chapter 4

1. How does a learning focus on the part of employees help an organization's customers?
2. How do adults learn differently from school-age students?
3. How does the learning environment impact the ability to learn?
4. How can you customize training and development activities to the needs of the trainee?
5. Why is feedback critical to learning?

Actions from Chapter 4

1. Identify the leader from whom you learned the most. What did he or she do that helped you learn? Practice two of these skills with other organizational members.
2. Write some questions about yourself and ask them of a friend. Include questions on the following:
   A. Communication skills.
   B. Willingness to receive feedback.
   C. How you deal with conflict.

3. Design a learning plan for yourself. Consider the following:

   A. Selecting a mentor.

   B. Setting reading goals.

   C. Soliciting feedback.

   D. Joining or starting discussion groups.

   E. Attending at least one external seminar per year.

   F. Taking college classes.

4. Identify the critical behaviors required for your organization's and your personal success. Rate your performance on each of these variables.

5. If you have not received formal documentation of your performance in the last year, make an appointment with the person to whom you report and share the above self-assessment. Then ask your supervisor for his or her evaluation.

5

Team Developer

The Nature of Teams

The popularity of teams in organizations is growing. However, teamwork has been described as a contradiction in American society (Weisbord, 1987). Tocqueville (Bella, et al. 1985) described the American tendency toward "individualism." Teams in the workplace are not implemented to limit individualism, but rather to capitalize on this creativity and add synergy to the group. Today, teams have been lauded for increased worker input on and ownership of daily tasks and decision making, improved quality of worker output, and improved customer service. A number of case studies have documented these successes and many others (Mohrman, Cohen, & Mohrman, 1995; Wellins, Byham, & Dixon, 1994).

Hindrances to teams include the need for quick decisions, the ongoing technical and social training required to enable teams, the higher skill level required to deal with inter- and intrateam conflict, the logistics of meeting times, the size of the team, information flow to the team about customer needs, the perceived threat to management, the speed of business in today's environment, and the perception of teams as democratic structures. Decision making takes more time in teams than in the traditional decision-making structure. It is obvious that the more people you include in the decision discussion the longer the decision making takes. Training is critical for successful team interactions. In the traditional structure, supervisors and managers were intermediaries for communication and conflict. Unfortunately, many of them did not meet these needs adequately. However, the expectation was that communication and conflict were not the worker's responsibility. The logistics of meeting times are often stumbling blocks for teams. Teams that don't meet for problem solving or the sharing of information and issues are not functioning teams.

One of the most frequent mistakes made as teams are designed is making the team too large. The size of the team and consensus have an inverse relationship. The larger the team, the more difficult it is to reach consensus. With large teams some people's concerns are ignored, and the time needed to accomplish group decision-making tasks is dramatically increased. It is important to create mechanisms for information flow to the team about customer needs. The staying power and ownership of teams that are not connected to the customer are doubtful. Managers are often fearful that teams will make them irrelevant. There are many valuable functions to which managers can migrate and contribute to the organizational goals. Business today is moving at a head-spinning pace. This reality requires managers to be honest and open about emergency decisions. Managers must also question themselves as to whether a particular situation is truly an emergency. The final hindrance to teams is the perception that team structure makes the workplace a democracy. Within the team itself, the perception is accurate, although voting is counterproductive due to the potential splitting of the team on issues. Management, however, does not abdicate its responsibility and accountabilities. They are expected to move from a highly directive style to an enabling style.

Weisbord (1987) described four conditions for team success. First, teams are successful if the team members are interdependent, and each person has a stake in the outcome. Second, the organization's leadership must be willing to take risks to improve group performance. Third, all team members must agree to participate on the team. Fourth, the influence of each person must be equal. Otherwise, the team structure will simply impose another hierarchy on the group.

Numerous types of teams are available to organizational leaders. Four common types of teams are permanent work teams, cross-functional teams, problem-solving teams, and leadership teams.

Permanent work teams involve those who are actually doing the work. Cellular work teams are one example of permanent work teams. This team involves a small group of workers in close proximity with front to end customer responsibility. Business unit teams are defined as teams who fulfill their responsibilities like a business. They deal with vendors and customers and are responsible for profit and loss results. Sequential work teams are small groups of workers who have internal and external customer responsibilities. These teams are useful when the proximity of workers is difficult to modify. Communication and problem solving are important tasks for this type of team. Self-directed teams can be any of the team structures described here. Generally, the literature defines self-directed teams as work teams. These teams plan their own work, communicate their results to management, schedule their own overtime and vacations, and prioritize issues to be addressed. Self-directed work team members are often cross-trained and rotate among the various team tasks.

Cross-functional teams involve members of several departments. The purpose of a cross-functional team is to produce a plan, complete a project, or solve a problem. Four questions need to be answered to determine the makeup of a cross-functional team. First, who has the pertinent information on the problem or desired product? Second, who will be impacted by the problem's solution or the team's final product? Third, who has the willingness and time to be on the team? Finally, who will have to carry out the group's decision? The team's makeup must represent the constituencies described in the questions. The cross-functional team must have a clear mission statement and defined parameters.

Problem-solving teams are subgroups of the larger team that meet separately to gather data and deal with a particular problem. The life of this team is only as long as needed to address the problem at hand. They report back to the entire team with their findings and recommendations.

Leadership teams include the top manager and his or her direct reports. The job of the leadership team is to involve all top managers in site decisions and to engender support for implementing organizational planning. This team is charged with supporting all other teams and establishing structures that enable the teams' success.

The chaos of today's environment prescribes the use of teams. Creativity, communication, and employee ownership can be enhanced through teams. It is valuable to realize that the term *team* can represent diverse structures and that teams can accomplish very different tasks (Richardson & Ray, in press).

Team Breakthroughs

Some teams experience almost magical breakthroughs that move them rapidly toward high performance. I realized a team breakthrough as a member of my high school football team. We experienced a dismal losing season my freshman year; we lost every game. The following two years were more successful, but there was always something that held the team back. Halfway through the first game of my senior year, the team's spotty performance seemed to be repeating itself. During halftime, the team lamented the 0–8 score in our opponent's favor. Our coach helped us understand that we weren't playing up to our potential. He also pointed out the basics of administering our plays that were missing. The coach gave us the confidence to accomplish our goals. At the end of the halftime, we went back on the field believing that we could beat our opponents, and we did. In the second half, we concentrated on our individual tasks in concert with other team members. We encouraged each other and focused on our goal. The final score was 22–8, our first victory of the season. We proceeded on to an undefeated season, the first in our school's history. Our coach served as a facilitative leader and enabled a team breakthrough that lasted the entire season. We were a different team going onto the field for the second half than we had been coming off the field at halftime. Many of us have experienced individual breakthroughs such as learning how to ride a bicycle or the moment when algebra finally made sense. These types of breakthroughs are common in our lives. It takes more effort and coordination to create a team breakthrough. The facilitative leader is vital for enabling team breakthroughs.

Team crises can create team breakthroughs. While working in the coal mines, I experienced two situations that immediately gelled a team. One situation occurred when a miner was injured and had to be carried out of the mine. The other situation resulted from a mine fire. In both cases, all team members dropped their personal conflicts and historical battles and worked together as a well-oiled machine. The facilitative leader enabled the team's success by repeatedly drilling them on the actions to take in such emergencies.

Encouragement of team members by the facilitative leader is similar to blowing on the embers when trying to start a fire. Because of the delicate nature of the first steps of a team, some teams take a lot of energy in order to become a well-oiled unit. Other teams take off like dry kindling, similar to the football team described earlier.

- Be a good listener.
- Keep an open mind.
- No cheap shots.
- Participate in the discussion.
- Ask for clarification.
- Give everyone a chance to speak.
- Focus on the present and the future, not the past.
- Deal with particular rather than general problems.
- Don't be defensive if your idea is criticized.
- Be prepared to carry out group decisions.
- All comments remain in this room.
- Everyone is an equal in this session (no titles).
- Be polite—don't interrupt.

Once everyone has had a few moments to read the list and make two selections, I ask for a volunteer to share the most important ground rule that he or she chose. In response to the team member's choice, I ask a follow-up question or tell a story that relates to the ground rule. For example, when team members suggest "Be a good listener" or "Keep an open mind," I ask the question, "What do you see when you see someone you judge to be a good listener or open-minded?" I keep asking questions until the team member describes behavioral observations. Some behavioral observations of listening might be, "Looks at me", or, "Writes down what I say". Some behavioral observations for open-mindedness may be, "Makes positive statements about my comment", or, "Gives me some time".

When "No cheap shots" is listed, I mention that there is a difference between having fun with a team member and taking cheap shots. Most team members agree. I also share with the group that I want to have fun at work. Again, generally, the team members agree. Next, I ask, "When does good-natured ribbing turn into a cheap shot?" Someone acknowledges that the turning point is different for each person. However, if we are paying attention, we can see when that turning point occurs. The insulted individual may move back from the table or reduce the number of comments that he or she had been making. If we feel that a peer has taken a comment as a cheap shot, it is our obligation to talk to that person about it, apologize for the insult if necessary, and eliminate that behavior in the future.

Some people know the hot buttons of others in their team and push them regularly. I once knew a mechanic named Timmy in the coal mine who was an expert in locating and pushing others' buttons. One day Timmy, Leroy, and I were eating lunch and Timmy leaned over to me and said, "You know, I can make Leroy throw up." I protested, "So? I don't want to see that." He ignored my protest and proceeded to make some well-planned comments to Leroy. In a matter of moments, Leroy's eyes became big as saucers, and he slapped his hand over his mouth and ran out of the lunch area, true to Timmy's prediction. I was stunned that he could or would do this to Leroy. I exclaimed, "What gives you the right to do this to Leroy just because you can? He is down here just like you and me, trying to make a living for his family." Timmy looked at me and said, "It's not my fault. If he can't take it, he shouldn't be down here." He blamed Leroy for being vulnerable. People who regularly throw cheap shots at others sometimes have the same view of life as Timmy. They feel no responsibility for the pain they inflict on others. I believe that we have an obligation to consider how others receive our humor and act respectfully based upon their responses.

Another ground rule, asking for clarification, is often suggested. I ask team members if they have ever left a meeting without knowing what was explained or expected of them. I usually see numerous heads nodding, so I follow up with the question, "Why does that happen?" Someone might respond that he or she didn't want to appear stupid. Then I ask, "Where did we learn that asking a question could result in our appearing stupid?" Invariably someone describes being scolded by a teacher or parent for asking a question. Then I share my experience with my third grade teacher, Mrs. Steed. I had just moved from Kentucky to Ohio and this was my first day at Beallsville Grade School. As I hadn't yet been fitted with eyeglasses, I didn't realize that my eyesight was bad and that I couldn't see as well as the other children. When Mrs. Steed wrote an assignment on the board, I made the mistake of asking her about it. I was just brazen enough to ask her to repeat the assignment. She replied, "What is the matter with you, can't you read?" As a result of her remark, I felt about an inch high. I asked very few other questions during the rest of that school year. I still think of that experience from time to time. Most of us have had a similar experience. The problem is that not asking questions can lead to mistakes resulting in bad products or unsafe situations. Team members need to be committed to asking and answering questions of other team members.

"Focus on the present and future, not the past," is a very popular ground rule. The reason this is an issue with many team members has to do with resistance to change (see Chapter 2). Others suggest that the reason we are unable to meet this ground rule is explained in Bruce Springsteen's song, "Glory Days." The song describes two high school friends who meet and automatically start talking about high school baseball as if it was just yesterday. To some people, the past always seems more real than the present. I had one such employee in a training session in 1986. We were talking about change issues in the company at that time. He kept making comments refuting the possibility of change, such as, "Supervisors will never listen to us. They never have for thirty years. Even if they do, they'll take our ideas and claim them for their own. We'll never get any credit." I listened and paraphrased the thoughts of this employee. The resistant employee asked the rest of the group for illustrations of their experiences with supervisors. Most described being aware of significant changes in the way supervisors interacted compared with their behaviors of five years before. I turned back to the resistant employee and made an observation while posing a question: "I can see that the experience that you are thinking about really hurt you. I can also see that it makes you angry even today when you think about it. When did these events that you've been describing happen?" He thought for a few seconds, rubbing his chin, and then said, "1966 or 1967." He had taken this experience and put it in a safe, warm place deep inside. Every so often, usually in a meeting, he allowed it to surface with the same intensity of emotion that he had felt twenty years earlier. Later, even the resistant employee admitted that supervisory behavior was presently more positive and respectful. In fact, the supervisor that he had been talking about had retired five years earlier.

When "Deal with particulars rather than general problems" is chosen, I tell a story about my son. When he was young, he occasionally claimed that I was unfair. My response was not an argument but rather the question, "What exactly have I done that you are describing as unfair?" The answer to that question really got to the root of the issue and allowed for explanation or problem solving. However, some people use this questioning approach as a denial of the problem being identified. I recommend that you be cautious of the danger of closing down communication with this phrase. Just because someone can't give you an illustration doesn't necessarily mean that there isn't a problem. Give the other person some time to think about and describe the root cause.

The discussion around "Don't be defensive" is usually interesting. I ask if I would see a lot of defensiveness if I were in their organization for a period of time. If the answer is, "Yes," I ask, "How do you know when someone becomes defensive?" Someone usually says, "He shuts up and doesn't say anything," or, "Her voice gets louder." I then self-disclose that the first thing I feel when I get defensive is my face flushing. Next, my jaw tightens and flexes. Finally, my voice rises and my eyes become like piercing lasers. These behaviors are physical manifestations of increasing adrenaline. I call this escalation "climbing the stair steps of adrenaline." I also self-disclose that never have good things happened to me at the top of the adrenaline stairs. One other point I make is that my choices are fewer the further I go up the stairs. That is why it is important to be aware of your nonverbal cues as you are climbing or beginning to climb the stairs. Finally, I ask the group if they know what their stair steps look like. Some do, but many don't. Addressing those who don't know their stair steps, I ask, "Who does know what your stair steps look like?" Answers come fast and furiously: spouses, children, parents, siblings, peers at work, and close friends. I suggest that they go to one of these people whom they trust and get some feedback on what the other people see as they become defensive or get angry. Once they find out this information, they can begin to take control of that part of their behavior.

A significant problem that teams encounter is a lack of follow-through on action items that are agreed on in team meetings. "Be prepared to carry out decisions" addresses this issue. I believe one of the reasons action items are not completed is that no one discusses why they weren't done. The team needs to analyze the contributing reasons why the action did not occur and then put remedial plans into place.

"All comments remain in this room" can be a useful ground rule or a strangling one. The key thing to keep in mind is whether comments repeated outside the room would hurt individuals on the team. Some comments could be useful learning to others outside the group and might be important to share. If the comments would have hurtful consequences, they should not be shared outside the team.

"Everyone is an equal in the room" is a ground rule that is important to many people. The fact is that we are not equal on any variable. You are taller or shorter than I and either heavier or lighter than I. The point of this ground rule is that we each deserve equal opportunity to be heard and treated as a valued member of the group.

Once the list is completed and discussed, I ask the team, "Is there any ground rule on the flip chart that you either can't or won't act in accordance with? If there is, you have veto power and we strike it off the list. This list is a living document. It should hang at every team meeting and members can add to or delete ground rules at any time as long as the team discusses the addition or deletion." I make these statements because the ground rules are only useful as a team tool if the team members own and obey them.

The next exercise in the interpersonal communication module is the Best Communicator Exercise. I ask the participants to think of a communicator whom they would describe as the best communicator they have personally known. Then I ask each team member to write down three behaviors that this person demonstrates that made the team member think of him or her. With this list we are focusing on the team members' perceptions of positive and desirable communication behavior. Once the list is complete, I ask the team members to look at it and choose one behavior they would like to work on personally after the session. The rest of the interpersonal communication module follows the material and points made in Chapter 3.

Group Development

The group development module begins with an icebreaker. The one that I most enjoy I call "To Tell the Truth." Each team member writes four statements about himself or herself. Three of the statements must be true and one must be false. I begin by demonstrating the technique with my own four statements. Some that I typically use are as follows:

1.   My mother was a "Rosie the Riveter" during World War II.
2.   I raised grand champion Jersey cows.
3.   I speak three languages.
4.   My grandfather was born in 1864.

After I read off the statements, I ask each team member to choose the one he or she thinks is a bluff. Then I identify the bluff and tell the team about me and my statements. It so happens for me that number three is the bluff. I got through French in high school and college but am not fluent. To be able to speak three languages is a future goal of mine. As for the rest of the statements, my mother was a "Rosie the Riveter" during World War II. As a young woman in her early twenties, she traveled from Crossville, Tennessee, to Utah to patch downed U.S. airplanes in support of the war effort. I did raise grand champion Jersey milk cows. For three years in the mid-1960s, my cow September Morn was the Grand Champion of her breed at the Monroe County Fair in Woodsfield, Ohio. My grandfather was born in 1864. He was a muleskinner hauling logs from Bowling Green, Kentucky, to

Nashville, Tennessee. He died at age 39 in a logging accident. My father was born in 1899. He was fifty-three when I was born, and he kept on till he got it right because I have a younger brother.

That is an example of the type of information that is shared by each team member during this icebreaker. Each team member has the opportunity to choose the level of self-disclosure with which he or she is comfortable. After everyone goes through the same process I just demonstrated, I ask the group how participating in this type of exercise changes the communication in a group. Some common responses are that they know one another better or see other team members more as people rather than just as fellow workers. Others are surprised at the diversity of experiences and interests of their team members. Several future conversations are usually launched as a result of this exercise.

Another segment of the group development module is to develop the team mission statement. The format that I use is dissected into three parts as follows:

To:

In a Way That:

So That:

The "To" segment describes the "what" part of the mission statement or the activity in which the team will be engaged. The "In a Way That" part of the mission statement focuses on the process aspect of the team's mission and explains how the team wishes to interact. The final mission statement segment, "So That," is the results part and defines the purpose of the team. I have each team member write down his or her thoughts on all three segments. Then I try to get all their thoughts captured on a flip chart. Next, I take the mission statement sheet and try to arrange the words in a grammatically smooth and flowing manner. This wordsmithing is done outside the training session itself. Later, I bring my proposal back to the team for their discussion, modification, and approval. A mission statement is useful for creating additional focus and direction for the team. The danger is that some teams spend too much of their most productive energy on producing the mission statement and have little energy left to accomplish the real task at hand. About 45 minutes are needed for the team to construct the first draft of the mission statement. Another half an hour a few days later is all that is needed to modify and approve the final version. As an example, the mission statement of my training group is:

To:	Provide effective communication-based training programs and employee development activities.
In a Way That:	Taps the creativity of our staff and our clients.
So That:	We enable our clients to improve their work relationships and better meet their customers' needs.

The third piece of the group development module is a facilitated discussion around the stages of team development described earlier in this chapter. Specific techniques to enable a team to move from stage to stage are described and demonstrated.

Fourth, the team behaviors and team members' roles are discussed and agreed upon. Lists of contrasting behaviors of traditional groups and teams are shared and explored. This contrasting list helps team members understand the scope and direction of behavioral change needed by all team members. The problem-solving and conflict management modules are described in Chapters 6 and 7, respectively.

Goal Setting

The fifth module, goal setting, creates motivation, defines common, clear, behavioral expectations, and helps team members to understand

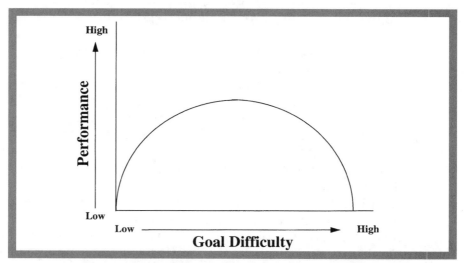

FIGURE 5-1. THE RELATIONSHIP OF GOAL DIFFICULTY TO PERFORMANCE

their role in the bigger picture. When setting goals, it is important to pay attention to four principles.

First, there is a curvilinear relationship between goal difficulty and performance. The goal must be challenging but within the vicinity of doability. If you set a goal just barely higher than your present performance, it is fairly irrelevant to motivation. You may have accomplished this goal without taking the time to perform a goal-setting exercise. One team set a goal of two and one half percent reduction in product rejects even though an upgrade on the piece of equipment that most contributed to rejects was scheduled. They probably could have made this goal with no additional effort or problem solving. Some organizations experience this type of goal setting because failure to reach one's goals is unacceptable and career threatening, so organizational members make the goals impossible to miss. On the other hand, goals that are totally unreachable are also irrelevant to motivation. People tend to abandon them in favor of more attainable but possibly very different goals, so unreachable goals can produce scattered results. Different team members can end up moving in very different and contradictory directions. Some organizations have what they call "stretch goals," which are by definition very difficult. According to the first goal-setting principle, the best way to structure stretch goals is to break up the task into a series of progressive goals; then focus on the immediate goals rather than the ultimate goal.

The second goal-setting principle is that specific goals lead to higher performance than general goals do. "Do a better job" or "Improve performance" are not useful goals. A good question to ask is, If I were doing a better job, what would you see me do? You can set goals around the answer to this question.

Third, participation in goal setting is related to performance through goal acceptance and worker commitment. Ownership of goals is the most important component of goal achievement. Goals that are determined by others and handed to the team risk being neglected by team members. If you ask a team to develop goals, make sure that they have adequate data to identify appropriate goals. Also, it is important to accept the goals the team selects. Once, as a supervisor in a coal mine, I was asked to develop some production goals for the upcoming year with my cross-shift supervisors. The three of us spent a Saturday looking at all the issues involved and making agreements among ourselves. Our section was one with particularly "bad top." Every time we mined the coal, the top would fall in, creating an additional number of tasks to perform. After our discussions we decided to set our production goal at an average of 80 feet of coal per shift. This was an ambitious goal for a difficult mining section. Our average production prior to the goal setting was about 60 feet of coal per shift. We proudly revealed our goal to our supervisor. Unfortunately, the response of our supervisor was that no goal less than 100 feet per shift was acceptable from any team of supervisors. My peers and I were deflated. We had hyped ourselves up to believe that we could actually accomplish a 30 percent increase in production. We came out of that session with less motivation than we went in with.

Finally, feedback about performance with respect to goals is important. Setting goals without providing adequate feedback is a problem. The facilitative leader shouldn't be looking over the shoulders of the team members. However, some regular checks between the leader and the team members should be planned. The frequency of these checks should be identified when the goal is set. With no feedback, the team may find that they have had a lot of activity but in the wrong direction. See Chapter 7 for more information about the structure of feedback.

The design of the goals can be accomplished with four questions: What, Where, When, and Who. The What question identifies the core of the goal and must be answered in relationship to the customer in mind. A review of the organizational vision and key strategies is important. It is valuable to give the team the top seven or eight parameters that drive your business. For expediency's sake, I like to break the team into two or three groups of three or four team members. Let each group choose a different variable on which to set a goal. The subgroup should decide what the desired outcome is and how much improvement on the variable is possible. It is valuable to give each subgroup historical data on the variable being considered. Finally, the subgroup should determine the steps required to accomplish the goal. An implementation flow chart is a useful tool at this point (see Chapter 6). Then I bring the team back together to share and discuss each goal proposal and come to consensus.

The second goal-setting question asks Where the team will focus their efforts. The Where question could be answered by identifying a particular piece of equipment or a particular plant location. The third question asks When the efforts will begin and When the results will be expected. The fourth question asks Who will be involved. At this point specific names must be attached to each event on the implementation flow chart.

There are three additional questions to consider: What measurements will the team use to determine its success? How will the team track and communicate its performance? What potential issues or roadblocks can be expected? Answering these questions can assist the team in successfully accomplishing their goals.

Expectations Communication

The seventh module is the expectations communication piece (described as a learning tool in Chapter 4). In the context of developing a team, it is the last training segment and ties all the other modules together. At this point the team has talked about their communication, how effective groups evolve and deal with problems, how to deal with conflict, how to use problem-solving tools, how to set goals, and what feedback is necessary. If this final session is well facilitated, a team breakthrough is not only possible but probable.

Summary

In this chapter, we explored a seven-step team development process. This model focuses upon improving the communication among team members. Other segments include group development, conflict management, meeting management skills, problem-solving tools, goal setting, and expectations communication.

Questions from Chapter 5

1. What is face time and how does it relate to team development?
2. What can the facilitative leader do to set the stage for a team breakthrough?
3. How do ground rules impact the team's communication?
4. Why is it important to allow team members to add or delete ground rules throughout the life of the team?
5. What is the difference between cheap shots and appropriate use of humor in a team?
6. How is goal difficulty related to performance?

Actions from Chapter 5

1. List the progressive behavioral stages that you demonstrate when you become defensive. Check the validity of these behaviors with a close friend or loved one.

2. Think about a team with which you are involved. Which steps of the team development model were adequately addressed? Which steps need additional work? Suggest to the team that some of the exercises recommended in this chapter be conducted to enable the team to be more successful.

3. If your team does not have a mission statement, use the format described in this chapter to write one with the entire team. Practice the technique by writing a mission statement for you personally.

4. Design a personal five-year plan for goals.

5. Write down your expectations of yourself and other team members. Suggest that other team members do the same and share the lists in a group.

6

Master of Problem-Solving Tools

The Problem-Solving Model

The fourth mode of the facilitative leader encompasses the mastery of problem-solving skills. We are not talking about solving problems for people, but rather enabling others to develop problem-solving skills. One develops new problem-solving strategies generated from the situation. This mode also results from the leader being a continual learner. Networking is important for the facilitative leader in order to tap the skills and experiences of a greater pool of employees. A focused employee solves problems by concentrating on what can be done rather than on what can't be done. Successful facilitative leaders desire to work with other organizational members to develop their potential for solving human communication problems.

The facilitative leader is action-oriented. I believe that this trait is an important part of problem solving. The phrase *action-oriented* reminds me of another story. When my two brothers and I were young, my grandmother had spells of ill health. During those times, she stayed in our home, and my mother took care of her. Her room was the downstairs bedroom next to the living room. On Saturday mornings, like most children in those days, my brothers and I glued ourselves to the television. Grandmother had a hand bell that she rang when she needed help. We were charged with equally dividing the task of meeting her needs. One Saturday, the bell rang. My older brother exerted his privilege of age, which meant he would go last. I jumped up and got Grandmother a glass of water. Later, the bell rang again. My younger brother was not eager to accept my older brother's logic, and an argument ensued. This argument interrupted my ability to enjoy the cartoons and, of course, there was a need to be met. So, I jumped up, helped my Grandmother, and was back in a flash. In a short while the bell rang for a third time, and I again jumped up and saw to her needs. My point here is that sometimes it makes more sense just to do something rather than to jaw it to death. I got more of my needs met—seeing more cartoons—by meeting my Grandmother's needs than by asserting my personal rights with my brothers. For problem solving to be viewed positively by employees, it has to result in some valued action or product.

There are four stages to the facilitative leader's problem-solving process. First, one must define the problem. Second, problem analysis is administered. Third, problem solutions are developed. Fourth, the solution is chosen and implemented. A substep to the problem definition and solution steps is the use of prioritization tools. There are a number of problem-solving tools that can be used for problem definition.

Defining the Problem

A useful tool to stimulate and capture creative thoughts for use in the problem-solving process is brainstorming. Four brainstorming formats are open, round robin, the affinity process, and the Delphi technique. Each format has unique characteristics for different populations. All brainstorming techniques should be prefaced by special ground rules:

1. Don't allow criticism during idea generation.
2. Think freely. No ideas are dumb during idea generation.
3. Develop as many alternatives as possible.
4. Build upon the ideas of others. Once ideas are posted, they belong to the group, not to individuals.

A note should be sent to every member identifying the topic to be considered and the purpose of the meeting well before the meeting begins.

Open brainstorming is administered by quickly recording ideas on a flip chart as they are shouted out by participants. It may be useful to have two flip charts so that the facilitator can move from chart to chart. All ideas should be encouraged. Sometimes it is useful to reframe the problem to break down mental barriers. The following two questions are examples of reframes: "What if you had all the money possible to address this issue?" "What if you had all the staffing needed to address this issue?" After the responses to the reframe are captured, the real-life parameters of the issue must be reimposed. Open brainstorming results in the most ideas, the most creative ideas, and the most synergistic flow of group interaction. The downside to open brainstorming is that individuals who are less verbal may not get their ideas on the flip chart. The ideas of dominant individuals might get the most attention, but there is no correlation between the verbal inclination of individuals and the quality of their ideas. Also, ideas from people of higher organizational status may influence the direction of an open brainstorming session.

Open Brainstorming

1. Define the brainstorming problem statement and write it on a flip chart. Place the problem statement in a prominent place.
2. Quickly record the ideas as they are shared spontaneously.
3. Continue listing ideas until all ideas are exhausted.
4. Reframe the problem statement (What if you had all the money possible to address this issue?).
5. Briefly discuss, clarify, and consolidate the listed ideas.

Round robin brainstorming is more structured. Each participant is asked to identify three (the number is arbitrary but should be small) ideas on the topic being brainstormed. Once the ideas are listed, each participant should prioritize his or her ideas. Then, the facilitator asks for the ideas one person at a time and continues gathering the ideas until all unique ideas are listed. Finally, discuss the ideas and consolidate those that are common. This technique is valuable for equalizing the input of all participants because highly verbal individuals can't dominate and status differentiation is leveled. Sometimes, when my boss or my boss' boss is in the session, I might hold back or inhibit my responses. This technique allows an opening for every participant. The downside is that it results in fewer ideas, the creativity suffers, and the synergy is reduced dramatically. Some of the synergy can be salvaged by suggesting that team members can, in turn, offer ideas that arise during the posting.

Round Robin Brainstorming

1. Define the problem and write it on a flip chart. Tape the problem statement in a prominent place.
2. Ask each participant to write down three ideas on the brainstorming topic.
3. Have each participant prioritize his or her ideas.
4. List one idea from each participant on the flip chart in their order of priority.
5. Continue listing ideas until all are exhausted.
6. Briefly discuss, clarify, and consolidate the listed ideas.

The affinity brainstorming process brings in several novel twists. First, ideas are generated and listed individually on sticky notes. Once all of an individual's ideas are listed, he or she then goes to a flat wall surface and spreads the notes across the wall. The next participant then places his or her notes on the wall. The additional notes that relate to other notes already on the wall are placed underneath the previous notes. This process of posting continues until all notes are on the wall. Next, all participants read the notes and rearrange them based upon relationships and themes. A few additional rules are important for affinity brainstorming. First, throughout the idea generation, posting, and theme development, there is no talking among participants. Second, once the notes go on the wall, they belong to the group, not the individual who identified the ideas. If there is disagreement on the placement of notes and they are moved between two theme areas several times, the facilitator places the note in controversy in a separate grouping. Finally, the theme lists are read by the facilitator and the participants name the themes with a title sticky note. The affinity brainstorming process creates a different product. It is most valuable for organizing vague problem statements and creating definition. Influence among participants is limited. Rather than gaining synergy, the group realizes the commonality of concern or beliefs about the problem at hand. The downside is that it is only useful with a small number of participants (seven or fewer).

Affinity Brainstorming

1. Define the problem statement. Write the problem statement on a flip chart. Tape the problem statement in a prominent place.

2. Ask participants to write down all their ideas about the problem statement on sticky notes.

3. Take the responses and place them on the wall in random order.

4. All members sort the responses by natural relationships.

5. Read the notes in each theme grouping.

6. Generate headers or titles for the themes that have been identified.

The Delphi technique developed by Dalkey (1969) is valuable for generating ideas even when participants are not together or even in the same country. First, the participants, called spokes, and the hub person are selected. Participants should be experts on the topic to be brainstormed. The hub person must commit to the most time consumption. All participants must be briefed about the process and agree to the expectations of the project. Then the topic is defined for the group and open-ended questions are constructed. Each participant responds to the questions posed. The hub person consolidates the responses into unique items. Then the items are returned to participants to be validated and to make sure no significant items are deleted. Once the list is validated, it is redistributed to the participants and they prioritize the items. This distribution and summary process continues until there is consensus among all parties as to the highest priority items to be implemented.

Delphi Technique Brainstorming

1. Define the problem to be addressed.

2. Choose an expert panel and a hub person.

3. Distribute an open-ended questionnaire on the topic.

4. Expert panelists complete the questionnaires and return them to the hub person.

5. The hub person consolidates unique items.

6. The hub person distributes a new questionnaire.

7. The expert panel prioritizes items.

8. A summary is sent to the expert panel for re-ranking.

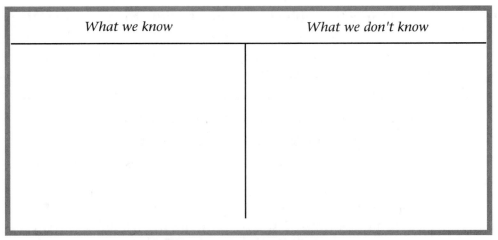

What we know	What we don't know

FIGURE 6-1. KNOW/DON'T KNOW CHART

Other tools that are useful during the problem definition stage are the Know/Don't Know chart and the Is/Is Not chart.

The Know/Don't Know chart is valuable for gaining consensus on the facts of a situation and on what data need to be gathered and analyzed. It is constructed on a flip chart by placing a big T in the center of the sheet. On the left side of the top of the T write Know, and on the right side write Don't Know. Use one of the brainstorming techniques described earlier in the chapter to fill in what the team agrees are the facts on the left side and the areas where data are needed on the right.

The Is/Is Not chart is constructed similarly to the Know/Don't Know chart. However, the purpose of this technique is to gain the team's consensus as to the parameters of the problem. The parts of the problem on which the team is willing and able to work are listed on the left side and those issues that are outside the scope of the team's abilities go on the right side.

Once the idea generation stage has been completed, prioritization must occur. Three prioritization tools are multivoting, payoff matrix, and Nominal Group Technique (NGT).

The multivoting technique helps a group reduce a large number of items to be considered in a way that tends to eliminate individual ownership of items. For an item to progress to the next round of vot-

	Is	Is Not

FIGURE 6-2. IS/IS NOT CHART

Items	1st Vote	2nd Vote	3rd Vote
A	7	5	0
B	3		
C	8	7	3
D	2		
E	4		
F	6	9	6
G	7	2	
H	5	0	
I	6	1	
J	6	0	
K	8	6	1
L	2		

Items C, F, and K, having received the most votes in the last round, are then equally evaluated with a payoff matrix.

FIGURE 6-3. ILLUSTRATION OF MULTIVOTING WITH TEN PARTICIPANTS

ing, it must receive a number of votes equaling or surpassing half the number of participants. For example, if there were ten participants in the session, the decision rule would be five. In round one, each participant may vote on all items he or she considers important. No more than one vote is allowed per item. In round two, each participant is allowed a total of three votes. The decision rule of five votes stands throughout the process. In round three, each participant receives one vote to distribute among the remaining items. Anytime a round results in three or fewer items, the process is complete and you move on to the payoff matrix.

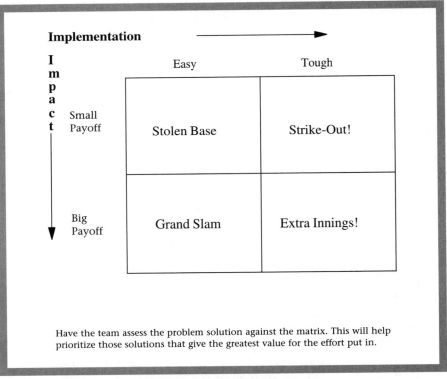

Have the team assess the problem solution against the matrix. This will help prioritize those solutions that give the greatest value for the effort put in.

FIGURE 6-4. PAYOFF MATRIX

The payoff matrix is a consensual discussion tool that fits neatly after a multivote. It is constructed of two bipolar decisions. One decision is based upon implementation of the alternatives at hand, easy or tough. The other decision regards the impact of the action being considered, small payoff or big payoff. The items that are the three finalists from the multivote are individually tested against these two questions. The result of the discussion is that the three items are placed in separate quadrants. The priority of action is prescribed by the quadrant chosen. First priority is given to items in the easy to do, big payoff quadrant. The small payoff that is easy to do may be a no-brainer and is probably next to solve. The third priority would be the big payoff that is tough to do. Before you begin work on the fourth quadrant, (tough to do with a small payoff,) you may want to focus on a new set of priorities. The energy required to complete an item in the fourth quadrant may not be worth the effort.

The beginning of the Nominal Group Technique (van de Ven, 1973) is basically a round robin idea generation process. Once the ideas are all posted on a flip chart, the ranking portion of the technique begins. First, the group members silently and independently rank order the top five ideas with the most promise. Second, the group members report and discuss their rankings. Third, another silent and independent re–ranking of ideas takes place by group members. Finally, group members report and discuss their final idea rankings, and the group seeks to come to consensus on the listing of solution ideas in rank order.

Another useful problem definition tool is the process map (see Figure 6-5). First, identify the process to be mapped. Second, define the beginning and ending steps of the process. Third, identify the outputs, the process' customers, and the inputs from the process' suppliers. Fourth, have each team member identify on separate sticky notes the individual steps to the process. Fifth, have the team members discuss the steps they have identified and arrange them in sequential order. Concurrent steps should be indicated.

This tool can be used for three purposes. First, you can map the process as you think it works by yourself. Second, you can map the process with other experts to determine how it really flows. Third, you can map the process as you would like it to be in order to optimally meet the customer's needs.

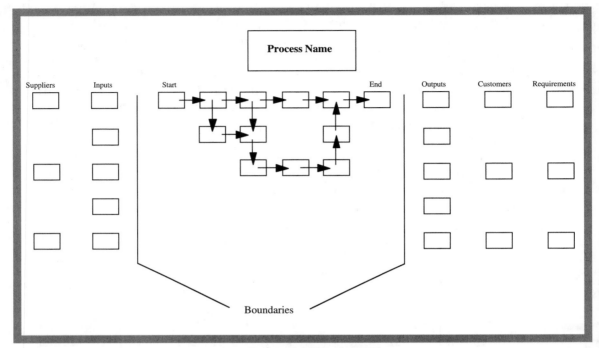

FIGURE 6-5. PROCESS MAPPING

Process Map

1. Identify the process to be mapped.
2. Define the beginning and ending steps of the process.
3. Identify the outputs and customers of the process.
4. Identify the inputs and suppliers of the process.
5. Ask each participant to write down all of the steps performed during the process on sticky notes.
6. Have participants discuss the identified steps and place them in chronological order.
7. Record any concurrent steps.

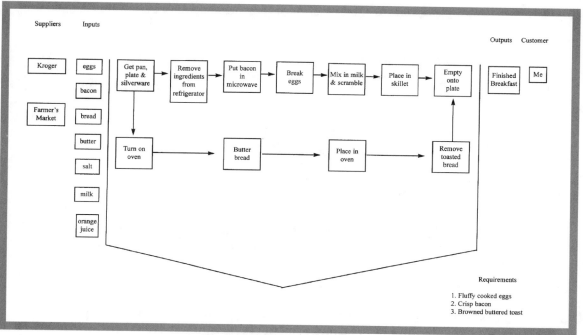

**FIGURE 6-6. PROCESS MAPPING
BREAKFAST PREPARATION**

Analyzing the Problem

Two problem analysis tools are the force field analysis and the cause and effect diagram. The force field analysis, developed by Kurt Lewin in the 1920s (Weisbord, 1987), is a tool that enables users to understand the opposing forces impacting a situation. All status quo situations in organizations are maintained by equally strong opposing forces. Driving forces move a situation toward change. Restraining forces hinder change. While both driving and restraining forces are identified in the process, only restraining forces are targeted for action. The analysis begins with brainstorming driving forces. Any of the brainstorming tools may be used. Then the process moves on to indicate the restraining forces. Once they are identified, the

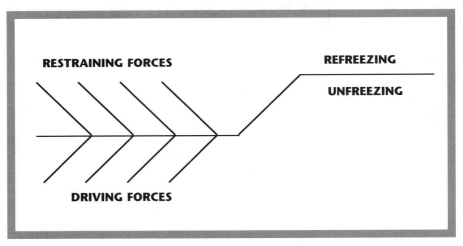

FIGURE 6-7. FORCE FIELD ANALYSIS

restraining forces are prioritized and action plans are developed. When the biggest restrainer is decreased, a process that Lewin called unfreezing occurs. *Unfreezing* means that the status quo is freed up to rise to a higher level of performance. Finally, the new status quo must be supported organizationwide to maintain the new performance level. Lewin called this support refreezing.

Force Field Analysis

1. Identify the situation to be analyzed.
2. Brainstorm positive driving forces of the situation.
3. Brainstorm restraining forces of the situation.
4. Prioritize restraining forces.
5. Problem solve and action plan the most important restraining force.
6. Institutionalize the change in the status of the situation through policy change, training, etc.

The cause and effect diagram is also called a fishbone diagram or Ishikawa Diagram (Evans and Lindsay, 1996). This tool organizes the potential relationships between a problem and its causes. Groups often jump to conclusions, assuming they know the cause of a problem before a full analysis is done. The tool is also helpful to identify probable root causes. The tool is called a fishbone diagram because it looks like one. The head of the fish is the problem or effect that is being analyzed. The four bones of the body of the fish are the four major sources of causes of the problem or effect. When manufacturing organizations use the cause and effect diagram, the bones are labeled with the four M's: materials, machinery, manpower, and methods. When service organizations use the tool, the bones are labeled with the four P's: policies, procedures, people, and physical plant. Another option is to brainstorm your own categories to fit your issue.

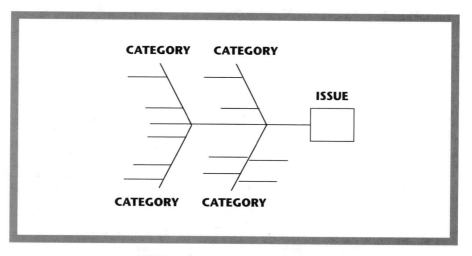

FIGURE 6-8. CAUSE & EFFECT DIAGRAM

Once the diagram is drawn on a flip chart, begin by brainstorming the causes under each labeled bone, using any of the brainstorming tools. When the causes have been identified, choose the bone that has the most impact on the problem or effect; use the payoff matrix to make this selection. Then use multivoting and a payoff matrix again to choose one particular cause. Next, analyze the individual cause with the Five Whys technique. The Five Whys consist of asking the Why question five times to get to the root cause.

Cause and Effect Diagram

1. Identify the situation to be analyzed.
2. Draw the fishbone diagram on a flip chart.
3. Brainstorm causes of the situation by bone or have facilitator place the identified cause on the appropriate bone.
4. Prioritize the causes.
   - Choose most significant bone.
   - Multivote items on that bone.
   - Administer payoff matrix to select final cause.
5. Ask Five Whys about final cause to identify root cause.

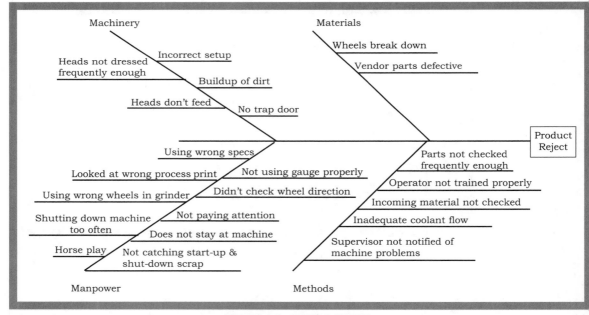

FIGURE 6-9. CAUSE & EFFECT
MACHINE SHOP REJECTS

The selection stage of the problem-solving process is similar to the problem definition stage. It is important to use different brainstorming tools to keep the interest of the team. The final stage of the problem-solving process is the implementation stage. Once you have selected a problem to address, action planning is necessary. PERT charts, flow charts, or Gantt charts are useful to plan your next steps.

PERT stands for Program Evaluation and Review Technique. Two critical concepts important to the PERT chart are milestones and activities. Milestones are events that have happened. If you travel the early roads in this country, such as the National Road in Ohio, you will see milestones that identify how much of your trip has been completed. PERT charts are useful to identify all of the steps or milestones of your implementation plans as well as time frames and critical paths. The activity is the doing of the task. Activities consume time. First identify the desired outcome. Then get the team together who will be responsible for the implementation. Have them write down the different milestones on sticky notes and then place the notes chronologically on a wall. The participants should have discussions about any disagreements that arise and come to consensus. Efforts should be made to identify any sets of tasks that can be accomplished concurrently. The result will be a diagram of the implementation plan. Next, estimate the times for each activity. Once that is accomplished, you can identify your critical path. The critical path is the sequence of activities that will take the longest total time. If you know the critical path of your plan and are asked to reduce the total time frame, you can add resources or efforts to the critical path to reduce the total time. Post this chart where all team members can track the progress.

PERT Chart

1. Identify the desired outcome.
2. Define the milestones involved in the project.
3. Determine the sequence of activities.
4. Diagram the milestones and activities into a network.
5. Estimate the times for each activity.
6. Identify the critical path.
7. Post the chart.

A flow chart is also a diagram of the sequence of events in an implementation plan but with the addition of decision points. Individual time frames are not often included in a flow chart. This tool visually represents in a focused way the steps to be taken. The tool also creates a common language and points of reference for talking about the implementation. First, identify the first and last steps of the implementation plan. Then identify the intermediate steps or tasks to be accomplished. Make sure complex steps are broken into separate

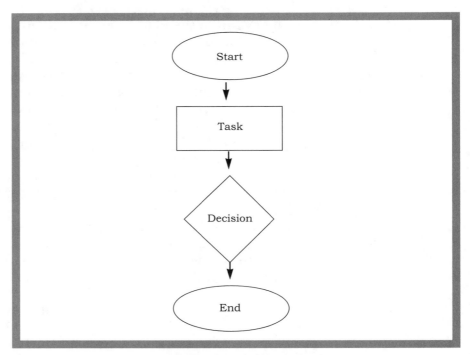

FIGURE 6-10. FLOW CHART

parts. Use rectangles to indicate tasks to be accomplished and diamonds to indicate decision points. Have participants write each step on a sticky note and arrange them all on a desk top, wall, or flip chart. Include feedback loops, sometimes called rework loops.

Flow Chart

1. Identify the first and last steps in the process.
2. Write all steps in the implementation process on sticky notes.
3. Break all steps down as far as possible.
4. Use rectangles to represent tasks and diamonds to show decision points.
5. Arrange the notes in a chronological flow.
6. Identify rework loops after negative decision points.
7. Post the flow chart in a readily accessible place.

The Gantt chart was developed by Henry L. Gantt, a protégé of Frederick Taylor (Baird et al., 1990). The Gantt chart illustrates the work planned and the work completed in relation to each other and to time. Potential work delays can also be shown. Each activity has its own timeline which is interrelated with all other activity timelines on the chart. The unique feature of a Gantt chart is that it diagrams the use of human resources at each phase of the project. The Gantt chart allows human resources to be optimized during the life of the project.

Resistance is a natural part of change. No significant change occurs without some resistance. The Stakeholder Commitment Chart enables participants to analyze the support for or resistance to the implementation plans by others inside or outside of the organization. This process can be used to identify the ease or difficulty of implementing a group's action plans. Once you understand the level of support for or resistance to your plans, a number of options are available. Some strategies to overcome resistance by stakeholders are to include them in problem definition, to engage in dialogue about the issue, or to negotiate modification of the implementation plan. The stakeholder commitment chart can also be used early in the team's life as you are identifying appropriate

STAKEHOLDER COMMITMENT LEVELS

| | LEVEL OF COMMITMENT | | | |
KEY PLAYERS	OPPOSED	NEUTRAL OR LET IT HAPPEN	HELP IT HAPPEN	MAKE IT HAPPEN
Plant Mgr				O X
Financial Mgr		X ◄──── O		
Engineering Mgr		O X		
Human Resource Mgr			O	X
Training Mgr				O X

FIGURE 6-11. STAKEHOLDER COMMITMENT CHART
(BASED ON A TEAM'S PROPOSAL TO BUILD A TRAINING
ROOM OUT OF A VACANT AREA OF THE PLANT)

organizational representation of team members to serve on a problem-solving team. Stakeholders include those who are responsible for the final decision, those likely to be affected by the outcome, those in a position to assist or block achievement of the outcomes, or those who have expertise or special resources that could affect the quality of the end product or service. Stakeholders are analyzed in terms of whether their minimum level of commitment to the implementation plans is to let, help, or make the proposed outcome happen.

First, draw the stakeholder commitment chart on a flip chart, as shown in Figure 6-11. Brainstorm the names of key individuals or constituencies whose commitment is absolutely essential and list them on the left-hand side of the chart. Make a decision as to the minimum level of commitment the group needs from each stakeholder in order for the proposal to go ahead. Place an O in the box that reflects that level of commitment. Next, make a judgment as to the stakeholders present level of commitment. Represent that level with an X on the chart in the appropriate box. If the X and the O are not in the same box, draw an arrow from the X to the O. This diagram becomes a map showing where work needs to be done to get the necessary commitment. Action is only required if the X is to the left of the O. When the X is to the left of the O, less commitment is present than is required to accomplish the project. The action plans could involve discussions with all critical players or bringing one key player before the group to discuss concerns.

Before you attempt to facilitate any new tools in front of your team, make sure you thoroughly understand the tool and have practiced it. It takes several administrations of a tool before a facilitator "owns" the tool or feels comfortable using it.

Sequence of Problem-Solving Tools

Problem-solving tools fit sequentially when analyzing an issue. Different tools fit more appropriately with certain problems. An example of four tools are illustrated on the problem stated as, "What are the barriers to broader demonstration of facilitation skills in this organization?" The tools described are round robin brainstorming, multivote, payoff matrix, and force field analysis.

In this problem-solving session there were ten participants. The problem was stated, clarified, and written on a flip chart so that the participants could refer back to it. Next, the round robin brainstorming technique was described. The participants were requested to independently write down three barriers on a sheet of paper at their tables. Once they completed the idea generation, the facilitator asked for a volunteer to identify the most important barrier of the three he or she had written down. The facilitator then started around the room retrieving one barrier from each participant until all of the ideas had been exhausted.

In order to begin the prioritization process, the multivote was used next. First, the tool was reviewed with the participants. The flip chart sheets were divided by lines into three sections. Each participant was given a sheet of red adhesive dots. They were informed that the decision rule for an item to be eligible to be voted on in the next round was the number of red dots equal to half the participants or, in this case, five. They were allowed to place no more than one dot on each item that they believed was important considering the problem statement. Ten of the fourteen items moved to the second round. Lines were drawn to identify which items were eligible for the second vote. For round two, each participant was given three blue dots to distribute among the ten remaining items. Four items received five votes or more. For the final vote, each participant was given one green dot which they placed on their highest priority barrier. Three items received votes. These items were the focus of the discussion using the payoff matrix.

The payoff matrix was drawn on the flip chart, and the three focus items—management hasn't bought in, wrong employees involved in decision making, and lack of understanding of facilitation—were written on sticky notes. The first question posed to the group was, "Would it be easy or hard to create management buy-in?" The group discussed the question and concluded that although top management supported the change, middle managers felt threatened by the process. Therefore, the group believed that it would be hard to change their minds. The second question was, "If this problem could be solved, would it make a big impact or a small one?" The group agreed that the support of middle managers would be critical to the implementation of broader demonstration of facilitation skills at the site. So, the first item was placed in the big-hard quadrant.

The next item considered was wrong employees involved in decision making. The group suggested that solving this issue would be fairly easy. It would simply require asking some simple questions such as: "Who would be impacted by this decision?" "Who has the information to make this decision?" "Who has the interest and time to make this decision?" and "Who has the power and resources to make this decision?" The second question was, "If this problem could be solved, would it make a big impact or a small one?" The group felt solving this issue would make a big impact on furthering use of facilitation skills. It would create successes in facilitated problem-solving sessions. These successes would create growing support among all employees. This item ended up in the big-easy quadrant.

The final issue was lack of understanding of facilitation. The group determined that it would be easy to solve with a small impact in comparison to the other issues. A briefing session with all employees explaining the process of facilitation and what they could expect in problem-solving meetings and answering any questions would meet this need.

The first item to address would be the big-easy, involving the right people in meetings. This could be done by designing steps to implement guidelines on employee selection for decision making and checking with employees to see if they believed the right people were involved. The second item is in the small-easy quadrant. This can easily be addressed and taken off the board. The third quadrant to be addressed is the big-hard area. This issue will require a number of other actions to take care of it.

To assist in analyzing the middle manager's resistance, the next tool to be used to increase the use of facilitation in the organization was the force field analysis. First, a brainstorming session was administered on the driving forces that put pressure on middle managers to support increased use of facilitation skills among employees. To identify the driving forces round robin brainstorming described above was used. Some of the drivers included:

1. Movements toward teams.
2. The amount of money and time spent in meetings.
3. Custom facilitator training sessions offered by company.
4. Competitor's use of facilitation.

Once the driving forces are listed, nothing more is done with them. The next phase is to identify the restraining forces. A Nominal Group Technique (NGT) was used to create and prioritize the list. The first step in the NGT is round robin brainstorming. After the list was generated, several rankings were performed by the participants. Each item was given a letter.

1. A. Fear of loss of power.
2. B. Lack of appropriate skill set.

3. C. Fear of getting up in front of peers or subordinates.
4. D. Lack of time.
5. E. Fear of loss of control.
6. F. Lack of respect for employees' ideas.
7. G. Resistance to change.
8. H. Fear of job loss.

	1	2	3	4	5	6	7	8	9	10	Totals	Rankings
Power	8	5	4	3	6	7	4	4	6	6	53	3
Skill Set	3	4	8	8	7	6	8	6	8	6	64	1
Up front	2	8	7	6	8	8	5	7	2	4	57	2
Time	4	7	1	7	1	3	2	8	3	3	39	6
Control	7	3	5	5	2	2	3	3	4	7	41	5
Respect	6	2	6	2	3	4	6	5	1	8	43	4
Change	5	1	2	4	4	5	1	2	7	2	33	7
Job loss	1	6	3	1	5	1	7	1	5	1	30	8

The top restraining force was lack of appropriate skill set. At this point the meeting time had run out. Since the participants were from different company sites, it was logistically difficult to get them together at one place. Therefore, a Delphi technique was used to select how to address the primary restraining force. One participant volunteered to be the hub of the process to consolidate responses. An e-mail message was sent with the brainstorming question, *What are all of the things that can be done to address the lack of skill set problem with middle managers?* The first round was as follows:

Participant #1

1. Hire external trainers for in-house seminar.
2. Send employees to a seminar and have them train managers.
3. Hire coaches to help managers.

Participant #2

1. Give them a bonus if they learn how to facilitate.
2. Give them a training program.

3. Hire a professional facilitator for each site.

Participant #3

1. Train them.

Participant #4

1. Buy them scented markers and a flip chart.
2. Send them to training.
3. Encourage the plant managers to describe the business needs for facilitation skills.
4. Encourage the plant managers to give positive feedback to middle managers.

Participant #5

1. Assess present skill set of managers.
2. Design different levels of facilitation training.
3. Hire an expert to teach the sessions.

Participant #6

1. Communicate the whys behind the need for facilitator training.
2. Give them a book on the subject.
3. Give them opportunities to facilitate parts of the plant manager's meeting.

Participant #7

1. Train them.
2. Move them into roles where they can't hinder the process.
3. Tie their success in gaining facilitation skills to their raises.

Participant #8

1. Send them to sites where facilitation is performed to observe the process.
2. Make sure any new managers hired have the desired skill set.
3. Meet with them to discuss their fears about facilitation.

Participant #9

1. Send them to external training.

2. Hold training in-house.

Participant #10

1. Create an in-house facilitator network so they can learn from each other.
2. Visit other companies that use facilitation.
3. Reward those who gain facilitation skills.
4. Offer the manager's facilitation service to customers.

The responses were consolidated into a list:

1. Hire external trainers for in-house seminar.
2. Send employees to a seminar and have them train managers.
3. Hire coaches to help managers.
4. Give them a bonus if they learn how to facilitate.
5. Hire a professional facilitator for each site.
6. Buy them scented markers and a flip chart.
7. Encourage the plant managers to describe the business needs for facilitation skills.
8. Encourage the plant managers to give positive feedback to middle managers when facilitation skills are demonstrated.
9. Assess present skill set of managers.
10. Design different levels of facilitation training.
11. Give them a book on the subject.
12. Give them opportunities to facilitate parts of the plant manager's meeting.
13. Move them into roles where they can't hinder the process.
14. Tie their success in gaining facilitation skills to their raises.
15. Send them to sites where facilitation is performed to observe the process.
16. Make sure any new managers hired have the desired skill set.
17. Meet with them to discuss their fears about facilitation.
18. Create an in-house facilitator network so they can learn from each other.
19. Offer the manager's facilitation service to customers.
20. Send all managers to an external seminar.

Assess Current Skill Set	1	2	3	4	5	6	7	8	9	10	Totals
Hire external trainers for in-house seminar.	5	5	3			4				4	21
Send employees to a seminar and have them train managers.	4							5			9
Hire coaches to help managers.			4			3		4			11
Give them a bonus if they learn how to facilitate.			2			2		3			7
Hire a professional facilitator for each site.						5					5
Buy them scented markers and a flip chart.											
Encourage the plant managers to describe the business needs for facilitation skills.	3							2	5	5	15
Encourage plant managers to give positive feedback to middle managers when facilitation skills are demonstrated.		1			1	1		1			4
Assess present skill set of managers.	2			1			2		4		9
Design different levels of facilitation training.			1				1		3		5
Give them a book on the subject.	1										1
Give them opportunities to facilitate parts of the plant manager's meeting.							3				3
Move them into roles where they can't hinder the process.					2						2
Tie their success in gaining facilitation skills to their raises.				5							5
Send them to sites where facilitation is performed to observe the process.		2							2		4
Make sure any new managers hired have the desired skill set.					3						3
Meet with them to discuss their fears about facilitation.				4					1		5
Create an in-house facilitator network so they can learn from each other.		3			4		4			3	14
Offer manager's facilitation service to customers.										2	2
Send all managers to an external seminar.			5	2	5		5				17
Invent rewards.		4		3						1	8

This list was sent to the participants to validate that their ideas were accurately represented. Once the hub received the responses, one item was added: Invent ways to reward middle managers for gaining facilitation skills. This completed list was then returned to the participants for a ranking. They were asked to rank the top five items, with 5 being the highest ranking and 1 being the lowest. The results are shown on page 124. The decision was made to hire an external facilitation expert to develop an in-house training program for all middle managers. The session would be initiated by the plant manager addressing the business needs for the training program. In order to sustain the skill development and support the change efforts, a network of facilitators at each site would meet quarterly. This series of meetings represents the unfreezing of the force field analysis.

To review, the tools used to analyze this problem were round robin brainstorming, multivoting, payoff matrix, force field analysis which included an additional round robin brainstorming, Delphi technique, and action planning.

Meeting Management Tools

In order to use the problem-solving tools described here successfully, there are several simple meeting management tools and techniques to keep in mind. These techniques include the use of an agenda, closure questions, a meeting evaluation, and meeting minutes.

Agendas are obvious meeting enhancers, but they are frequently ignored or poorly administered. The purposes of a meeting agenda are to identify meeting topics, to provide structure, and to define expectations for the team members.

Here are seven tips for constructing and using meeting agendas. First, design the agenda prior to the meeting. The core of the agenda can be identified at the end of the previous meeting. E-mail is very useful for adding to or prioritizing an agenda prior to a meeting. The Delphi technique described earlier in this chapter is especially useful for this task. Second, seek input from participants. One person should be responsible for coordinating the agenda, but ownership by the group is most important. Making sure each team member has an opportunity to contribute to the agenda will create team member commitment to the agenda.

Third, include followup and unfinished items in the next agenda. These items need not maintain their same priority in the next meeting. One mistake that some teams make is to develop a to-do list and then proceed through the items using a first-come, first-served approach, without reevaluating each item against new items. The completion of one agenda item might impact the importance of other items. It is useful to discuss these relationships periodically.

Fourth, define on the agenda the time frame and responsible person for each agenda item. The time frames are estimates, based on the complexity and importance of the topic. It may be necessary to extend time frames depending upon how the discussion develops. Remember, the time frames don't drive the team; the team drives the time frames. Naming responsible parties for specific items helps reduce confusion about who needs to prepare for what. The fifth tip is to distribute the agenda in advance of the meeting. Again, this is easily done using e-mail. If your organization doesn't have an e-mail system, distribute hard copies. The problem with handing out the agenda when everyone arrives at the meeting is lack of preparation by some members. I remember arriving at a meeting years ago with the other team members. The meeting leader handed out the agendas, and two team members excused themselves so they could go back to their offices to retrieve needed files. Had they known of the topics to be covered in advance, they could have brought those files in the first place. The sixth tip is to display the agenda in a prominent place. I like to put the proposed agenda on a flip chart sheet and tape it to the wall so all team members can observe the team's progress and adherence to the time frames. Finally, review the proposed agenda at the beginning of the meeting. Feel free to modify the agenda to meet the most pressing needs of the team.

Once the meeting agenda items have been addressed or the time has run out, there are several closure items to deal with. First, review and summarize any decisions that were made during the meeting. Second, if several decisions are made at each meeting, it may be useful to have a flip chart sheet so decisions can be listed as they are made. The decision list can also help in assuring consensus or generating discussion when consensus is in doubt. This process can ensure that all members are "on board" with the decisions that are made. Third, discuss next steps or potential follow-up work. Fourth, assign responsibility for necessary tasks for the next meeting, such as minutekeeper, timekeeper, scribe, and the person responsible for logistics. The minutekeeper adds his or her notes to the key decisions chart. The timekeeper is not the time police, but simply lets the team know when the allotted time has run out. The team members then decide whether to continue the discussion or wrap up the item and proceed on with other agenda items. The scribe's job is to capture decisions made or key points discussed on the flip chart for further use. The logistics person makes sure that the meeting room is available and scheduled and that a flip chart and markers, overhead projector and screen, or other needed meeting materials are handy in the meeting room.

Fifth, determine the time, date, and location for the next meeting. This scheduling is much easier to handle when everyone is together with their calendars open. Finally, identify known agenda items for the next meeting. These items can be circulated via e-mail so others can add to them.

At the end of a team meeting it is important to evaluate with the team members the progress or lack of progress. The evaluation technique can be simple or complex. One of the simplest evaluation techniques is to ask team members to share one thing that they liked about the meeting and one thing they might change about the meeting. Some teams have developed evaluation tools with five-point scales around the team's ground rules or elements of the team's mission statement. It is important to change the evaluation items occasionally. After repeated use of the same evaluation form, team members can become bored, and the results can be less useful.

Example evaluation tool constructed from team ground rules

	Met Completely				Didn't Meet
1. Everyone was treated equally.	5	4	3	2	1
2. Ideas were valued.	5	4	3	2	1
3. We focused on the most important issues.	5	4	3	2	1
4. We listened to one another.	5	4	3	2	1

Minutes are an important documentation of the product of a team meeting. With every meeting, the team and the company are purchasing something. One of the costs incurred with a team meeting is the salaries of the team members consumed by the meeting. Sometimes overtime costs are involved for replacements back on the job. The facilities where the meetings are held carry an overhead cost. The materials used during the meeting add to the costs. The team and company also lose opportunity costs, or the value added activities the team members could be delivering to their customers instead of attending the meeting. If you aren't willing to document your meetings, you don't have the right to convene a meeting (Kayser, 1990). Once you add it all up, the cost will surprise you.

Many times taking the minutes of a meeting and distributing them are considered painful and laborious tasks. To reduce the pain, keep the minutes as simple as possible. Never take minutes that are more than one page in length. List the date of the meeting, the participants, the decisions made at the meeting, and the actions to be taken, including time frames and responsible parties.

Summary

In this chapter the problem-solving aspect of the facilitative leader was described. A four-stage problem-solving process was developed. A number of problem-solving techniques that the facilitative leader uses were described. These techniques included open, round robin, affinity, and Delphi brainstorming tools; know/don't know and is/is not charts; multivoting, payoff matrix, and Nominal Group Technique prioritization tools; the process map; the force field analysis; the cause and effect diagram and Five Whys; PERT, flow, and Gantt charts; and stakeholder commitment charts. Finally, effective meeting management techniques were described.

Questions from Chapter 6

1. Which technique, open or round robin brainstorming, would you use for the following participant characteristics and situations?
    A. Highly verbal participants?
    B. Participants with low verbal inclination?
    C. Status differentiation?
    D. Need for creativity?
    E. Need for volume of ideas?
2. What are the problem-solving tools that are incorporated in the force field analysis?

3. How does the stakeholder commitment chart help a team implement their problem solution?

4. Why might it be important to not address brainstormed problems in the order that they were originally prioritized?

5. What is the timekeeper's role in the problem-solving meeting?

6. Why is it important to use a variety of meeting evaluation formats?

Actions from Chapter 6

1. Identify a problem with which you are dealing and design a map for using a sequential series of problem-solving tools to address the issue.

2. Think about how agendas have been used in past meetings in which you have participated. List the positive and negative aspects of their use.

3. Design three different evaluation tools for your team meetings.

4. Identify the various costs that your organization pays for holding meetings.

5. Choose an appropriate problem-solving tool to be used in your next team meeting. Review the tool and identify the steps you will use in as much detail as necessary. Don't underestimate the complexity of the tool.

7

Manager of Conflict

Feelings about Conflict

One job of the facilitative leader is to deal with conflict as it arises among group members. The difficulty of accomplishing this task varies tremendously by group. When developing facilitative leaders, it is productive to begin the discussion by exploring how individuals feel about conflict. Break the group members into small groups of four and ask them to draw pictures on a flip chart that describe their feelings about conflict. In my sessions, examples have varied from a sun and people shaking hands to lightning bolts and arrows through the head.

The picture of the sun described the creativity that can come from conflict. The picture of people shaking hands resulted from the relationship growth that often accompanies successful conflict interactions. The lightning bolts and arrows indicate the pain that we frequently feel during and after conflict. Conflict can sometimes be scary. In fact, one group of participants drew a scene of a stick figure struggling up a hill, pulling on a rope that was wrapped around a house. Another rope was being pulled in the opposite direction by three other organizational members. Some team members feel that

DRAWING BY BERNIE MUIZNIEKS

FIGURE 7-1. PICTURES OF CONFLICT

FIGURE 7-1. PICTURES OF CONFLICT

DRAWING BY BERNIE MUIZNIEKS

It is as natural as a river flowing. The river is in conflict with the earth.

FIGURE 7-1. PICTURES OF CONFLICT

DRAWING BY JANICE THOMAS

conflict diverts energy from the real task, destroys morale, and polarizes individuals and groups while producing irresponsible behaviors. Another picture showed a river flowing through a meadow lined with trees with the caption, "It's as natural as can be." The creator of this picture explained that there is constant erosion created by the river's conflict with the earth itself.

During the overview discussion about conflict, I ask the following question: If I had a bottle of Ray Ray No. 9 and gave each person in your organization a squirt, with the result being the elimination of all conflict, would you buy a bottle? The first reaction of many people is, "Of course, I'll take a gallon." I then add a second element. Not only will Ray Ray No. 9 eliminate conflict, but it will make everyone just like me. This twist generates a different response from the original question. Gradually, people acknowledge that the sameness and lack of disagreement would be boring and unproductive for their organization. Conflict will always be with us. It is important to realize that we wouldn't get rid of it if we could.

Conflict as a concept is neither good or bad. Conflict can be positive and useful. It can result in more creativity and better ideas and

FIGURE 7-1. PICTURES OF CONFLICT

solutions. Conflict can enable us to confront issues in an open manner. Issues are clarified, team members feel more involved, and communication is more spontaneous when disagreements are allowed and encouraged.

Groupthink

A potential negative outcome of eliminating conflict is called groupthink (Janis, 1972). The concept refers to groups whose individual members are not comfortable in speaking their minds or cultures that have a strong "don't rock the boat" mentality. The Bay of Pigs incident in the Kennedy administration was a famous illustration of groupthink. Robert McNamara and Arthur Schlesinger doubted the wisdom of sending an armed band of Cuban refugees to a Cuban beach without any support. While discussing their concern one day, Robert Kennedy, the Attorney General, heard their discussion. Kennedy reprimanded them as being disloyal to the President. He suggested that they put their energies into making this project happen, not criticizing the President. The outcome of this inability to disagree with a wrongheaded initiative resulted in our country coming the closest ever to nuclear war in our history—the Cuban Missile Crisis.

Another notable groupthink incident involved the Challenger shuttle disaster. The Reagan administration dearly wanted to talk about the space program and recent improvements in reliability and timeliness of flights in the State of the Union address scheduled for the evening of the explosion. Everyone at NASA realized the urgency and importance of this flight. Even though engineers at Morton Thiokol feared the consequences because of new data that had been generated, they refused to overturn previous launch temperature criteria. The results were disastrous.

Conflict Management Model

People list a variety of reasons why conflict occurs. Misunderstanding, personality clashes, perceptions about performance of teammates, differences in performance methods, and competition over limited resources are but a few reasons given for conflict. Misunderstanding may be the largest single creator of conflict. Based upon the small overlap of the fields of experience, the volume of misunderstandings makes sense. Labeling a conflict as a personality clash is often a way to dismiss it as unresolvable. Personality clashes are really the result of behaviors demonstrated by both parties. In order to deal with personality clashes, it is important to identify the behaviors that both parties are demonstrating that underlie the conflict. Then, you can make choices that can impact the conflict in a constructive way.

For example, at one plant where I worked, an engineer and a production manager were constantly arguing in a cross-functional meeting. When I approached the two men separately, each of them expressed little hope for improving their relationship because of a personality clash. Upon further questioning, I found that one individual repeatedly interrupted the other or shook his head while his peer talked. On the other side, the complaint was that commitments were made and not kept and that his peer smiled when he disagreed with him. As you can see, there were specific behaviors being demonstrated which each party responded to with anger. It is better to bring these behaviors to the surface to discuss and solve them rather than dismiss the conflict as a personality clash.

Perceptions about performance of other team members are often cited as reasons for conflict. Most of us go to work each day with the intention of doing a good job. However, our perceptions may not be in alignment with the perceptions of other team members. Some dialogue among team members regarding expectations as described in Chapter 4 is useful to clarify team member accountabilities. Another reason for conflict is differences in performance methods. Each of us develops our own way of accomplishing tasks. I have been told that at shift change in some chemical plants the oncoming team members automatically change the equipment settings first thing. Sometimes by making these changes the product is thrown out of acceptable quality parameters. To create consensus on performance methods, have cross-shift team members get together and create a joint process map of the work procedures. The dialogue from this session can impact the daily changes at shift time.

Competition over limited resources is an increasingly common reason for conflict. Resources have always been limited, but in the past the responsibility for managing resources belonged to a few top leaders. Today, each of us has to make decisions among several alternatives because of limited resources. If we gain resources, others lose them. Often it is not possible to satisfy everyone. However, if the expenditure of resources is determined based upon key organizational objectives, most team members can understand the choice.

Interpersonal conflict can be described as head butting, like two rams in rutting season. The conflict takes this turn because two people take conflicting positions and neither will consider the merit of the other person's proposal. We need to learn new ways of dealing with conflict, and this learning is possible. One approach to bring two individuals to agreement is described by Fisher and Ury (1991) in their best-selling book, *Getting to Yes*. The following material is based upon their work. There are seven components to the conflict management model:

1. Relationships
2. Communication   Environment Setting

3. Criteria
4. Interests and Needs   Problem-Solving Steps
5. Options

6. Commitment   Follow-up
7. BATNA (Best Alternative to a Negotiated Agreement)

The first two components, relationships and communication, are what I call environment setting. Relationships are critical to the possibility of solving a conflict and to the ability to get work done. Perceptions of trust, respect, fairness, and openness all describe the relationship's health and the potential conflict management environment. If the relationship is damaged, remedial work is necessary before conflict can be managed successfully. If you hate my guts, the probability that we can come to agreement is very low.

As we discussed in Chapter 3, relationships are defined by communication. If you feel respected by the way I communicate with you,

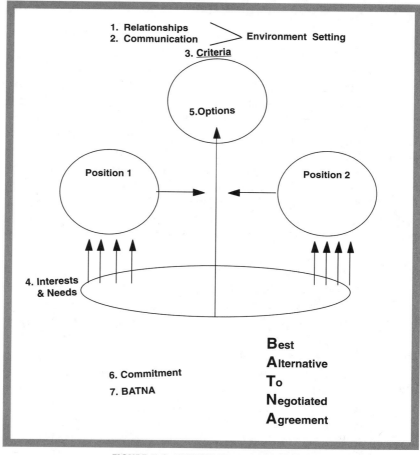

FIGURE 7-2. REACHING AN AGREEMENT

verbally and nonverbally, we will be more able to deal productively with our conflicts. The converse is also true. If we have a negative relationship, one option is to change our communication to a more respectful type. Another process to improve past communication relationships is called signposting. Signposting involves discussing a new interaction pattern with the other party.

Signposting Example

Lee, I'd like to talk to you about the way we communicate. I know that we have taken public verbal jabs at one another in the past. On this project we really need to work together. I intend to eliminate the public jabs and listen more completely to your ideas. How do you feel about us trying to improve the way we communicate?

I call the next three components the problem-solving steps of conflict management. First, determine the criteria for success. The criteria describe how the two parties will know that they have been successful in producing a win–win solution. They must be measurable. Once the criteria have been defined, the positions should be reviewed and then discussion on the positions should be suspended. Positions are the perceived mutually exclusive paths of action that different parties support. The next component is the needs and interests that underlie the position. This information should be the focus of the discussion. The appropriate question here is, "What needs or interests would you meet if your position was made reality? What do you hope to accomplish with that position? What would that position do for you?" You can also begin by sharing your needs and interests. The key objective is to uncover and discuss the needs and interests of both parties. Then, you can identify the commonalties between the two lists. Generally, people find that there are more commonalties than differences when you look at needs and interests, not positions. The third action step of the conflict management process is the creation of options or alternatives. Options concern all of the possible ways to meet both parties' interests. The options can be listed through brainstorming or some other idea generation method.

After the problem-solving steps, two other components are left to complete. This is the follow-up segment. The two final steps are to determine the level of commitment to the solution and to develop what Fisher and Ury call your BATNA (Best Alternative To a Negotiated Agreement). Of course, commitment is critical to the success of the action plans to resolve the conflict. A thorough discussion should be held to make sure that agreements are not superficial. Sometimes, failed commitments result from unrealistic action planning. Other times tasks are imposed on others without discussion. There is always some reason why the solution was not supported. Some failed commitment cycles repeat themselves because the poor performance is not acknowledged, discussed, or analyzed.

Finally, BATNA comes into play only if agreement cannot be reached. If it is clear that the two parties cannot come to agreement, this final step should be taken. After the discussion is over, both individuals will do something regarding the issue at conflict, depending on their power and available resources. The final communication on the issue involves each person telling the other what he or she will do, given that they could not come to agreement. If each party knows what to expect, everyone can make more effective decisions for the team and the organization.

Let's say, for example, Joe and Jack are both held accountable for developing training for their respective teams. They engage in a discussion on how to design and administer the training together. Unfortunately, they are unable to come to agreement. Joe wants training solely on interpersonal communication. Jack, on the other hand, is determined to design a conflict management training module. Once they see that agreement is not possible, each party should describe a next step or BATNA, things one can do without the other party. In this case they can each create separate programs. With this knowledge of future actions, they can also share the contents of the programs with each other. This information can help the organization in several ways. Jack may be able to incorporate some of Joe's program content in his training. After all, conflict is solved through communication. They can both learn from the success of the two programs and may choose to collaborate more successfully in the future. Failure in conflict management doesn't have to mean closure of the relationship.

Conflict Management Questions

There are several appropriate questions inherent to the conflict management process. First, during the environment setting, ask the questions:

> What is the status of the relationship of the parties in conflict?
>
> How can we improve the communication to enable conflict management?

In conjunction with the problem-solving segment, ask:

What needs would be met if we implemented your position?

What are you trying to accomplish?

How do the needs and interests of the two parties relate?

What options or alternatives do we have that will best meet the majority of the needs and interests of both parties?

Finally, during the follow-up segment, ask:

Are we really committed to accomplishing the chosen alternative?

A month from now, will anything prevent us from carrying through our commitments?

What are we both willing and able to do on this issue if we are not able to come to agreement?

These questions enable one to step through the process in a logical, productive fashion. The process can be used as a solitary analysis of conflict in which you are engaged, or two parties can use the process as a template to discuss their conflict with or without a neutral facilitator. The process is also useful to analyze conflict in which two other organizational members are enmeshed.

Let me share an illustration of one use of the process when my wife and I disagreed about our transportation needs. The position she had taken was that I needed a truck. My position was that I wanted to remain truckless and continue driving my Ford Probe. First, we looked at criteria with which to measure a successful solution. We decided that all future transportation options were on the table. However, we wanted our monthly outlay for vehicles to remain close to the present level, including total monthly car payments for two cars. Then we shared with each other the needs and interests that resulted in our different positions. I asked her what needs of hers would be met if I had a truck. She responded that she wanted improved haulability. She wanted to be able to haul a Christmas tree once a year, new furniture occasionally, and shrubs and trees for landscaping. I shared that my needs involved the feel of a pseudo-sports car, both being low to the ground and the projection of a sports car image rather than a truck. I also had an economic reason for my position: The Probe's gas mileage was better than most trucks, and I like economical cars because I drive more than 25,000 miles a year. During this discussion, we also realized that her convertible had some good points, but it rattled at every bump. We began visiting car dealerships and looking at our options. In the end we traded the convertible for a Mercury Villager minivan. With this solution, most of our haulability needs were met, we got rid of an undesirable vehicle, and I kept my Probe. The way we approached the dialogue allowed us to identify the unspoken underlying needs.

Conflict Styles Inventory

As a manager of conflict, the facilitative leader needs to be flexible in choosing conflict styles. I use the Thomas-Kilmann Conflict Mode Instrument to illustrate the different styles of dealing with conflict that members of a team have. The five styles that the Thomas-Kilmann instrument documents are competing, collaborating, compromising, avoiding, and accommodating (Thomas and Kilmann,

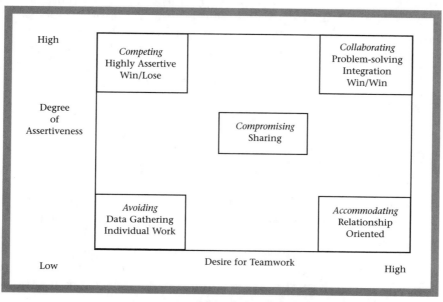

FIGURE 7-3. CONFLICT MANAGEMENT STYLES

1974). The five styles are defined by two scales that measure the variables of assertiveness and desire to work with others. I believe that each of these conflict styles brings some positive and some negative aspects to the team interactions.

The competitive facilitative leader is highly assertive, yet prefers to work independently. He or she often brings a push for excellence to the table, thus creating outcomes that are superior. A competitive leader continually assesses the team to determine appropriate timing for new challenges. Boredom will kill a team faster than anything else. A competitive leader will keep things exciting. The problem with the competitive leader is that he or she may steamroll other team members and damage future relationships. Through feedback one can raise the highly competitive leader's awareness of the damaged relationships and the future erosion of cooperativeness of team members that the aggressive approach creates.

The collaborative facilitative leader is also highly assertive but enjoys working with others. He or she knows when to bring the team together for synergistic problem solving. Some issues impact a number of people and the understanding of the problem varies across the team. This type of problem is a perfect opportunity for involving all members of the team in a problem-solving session. The collaborative facilitative leader tries to involve as many people as possible in the problem-solving process. The problem with this style of conflict management is that it takes more time than some other styles. Time is a precious commodity in today's work environment. The use of this style can create a backlash against the collaborative facilitative leader due to time pressures.

The compromising facilitative leader is at the midpoint on both the assertiveness scale and the desire to work with others scale as shown in Figure 7-3. He or she knows when to split the difference and when to compromise. This conflict management style is probably the most time-efficient style of all five. When time is of the essence, compromising makes sense. However, the facilitative leader must be careful not to rely too heavily on this style. It could result in the lowest common denominator winning out, as illustrated by the U.S. Congress. Republicans offer an initiative that may create some positive outcomes for the country. Democrats offer another initiative that, if implemented, might create some positive outcomes for the country. They get together and compromise until the final solution is so watered down that it does little for anyone.

The avoiding, or as I call it, deliberate, facilitative leader is low on the assertiveness scale and prefers to work alone. This leader is not one who doesn't take action but who does like to think the issue over. The avoiding leader does, however, take more time than any of the other styles. The positive contribution of the avoiding leader is that he or she doesn't jump into a conflict situation when the situation could resolve itself. I remember when I first became a supervisor in my twenties. Anytime a conflict occurred, I felt the obligation to jump in and try to solve it for the participants. Sometimes by taking this action, I made the situation worse than if I had stayed out of it. The avoiding leader likes to mull the situation over for a while and sleep on it. He or she likes to gather more data on the issue before taking a stand. I am an avoider when it comes to buying a car or a house. When my wife and I go to a car lot, she makes split-second decisions about her likes and dislikes on this car or that car. Finally, she'll spot a car and exclaim, "This is my car! I want this car!" I insist that we visit every dealership in the county and think about our decision for a while. In every case we end up going back and buying the first car she chose. She knows what she likes. The avoiding facilitative leader knows when to do nothing. Some issues, given a little time, will resolve themselves. The facilitative leader does not jump in if the team can handle the problem themselves. From my experience, this is the most common conflict style of supervisors and managers. This may result from organizational reinforcement of leaders who do not take rash actions.

The final conflict management style of the facilitative leader is the accommodator, who is low on assertiveness with a strong desire to work with others. This person is the social glue of the organization. He or she is more interested in the ability to work with other team members in the future than in the outcome of the current conflict itself. The accommodating facilitative leader knows when to take the time to focus on relationships. Of course, as the team is assembled or as new members come and old ones go, specific team-building steps must be taken to create an effective team. At other times in the team's life, it is important to refocus on the contributions and individual talents and skills of all team members. Some of these times may occur after an especially intense sequence of work or after solving an emotionally charged issue. Icebreakers that include some level of self-disclosure, or adventure team-building that gets the group away from the traditional team environment, are two ways to refocus on the team relationship. The problem with this conflict management style is that the accommodating leader may feel taken advantage of and negative toward others after the conflict discussion. He or she may also accept a less than optimal solution for the sake of the relationship.

I don't prescribe one style over another. It is important, however, to understand the strengths and concerns of each style and to try to capitalize on improving your strengths. Each person generally has more than one favored style. The effective facilitative leader knows when to switch style to match the situation and the people involved. However, if the organization's culture forces you to interact in an unfavored style, you will be very stressed.

Feedback

One of the reasons for conflict in groups is a lack of feedback among group members. Disruptive behaviors are perpetuated by the lack of communication about the undesirable behavior. Positive feedback can head off future relationship problems and clarify expectations. I suggest a two-phase feedback process. First, deliver an "I message." Then focus on specific desired behaviors and the business needs. The "I message" describes the event of the feedback and the feedback sender's feelings about the feedback event.

Positive Example

"Yesterday when **you taught me the new spreadsheet software** (event), I **felt pleased** (feelings) that you took the time to help me understand it completely."

"I messages" are strongly owned statements by the sender that are behavioral and objective. They focus on demonstrated behaviors, not personal evaluations. The second segment concerns specific desired behaviors and the business needs.

Positive Example

"In the next week I would like you to **show me how this spreadsheet can be incorporated in our newsletter** (specific desired behavior). If you can teach me this skill, I can take a turn every other month to edit our newsletter. That way you can **spend more time with our customers.**" (business need).

I call this whole process E-FAB Feedback:

What Event(s) have occurred about which feedback is important?

How do I **F**eel about the above event?

What specific future **A**ctions need to take place?

How will the future actions impact the **B**usiness needs? (The business needs can also be defined as personal or family needs.)

The E-FAB technique can be used for constructive feedback as well as positive feedback. I use the term constructive rather than negative feedback. Negative feedback feels like a slap in the face. Constructive feedback helps design a more effective alternative course of action.

Constructive E-FAB Feedback

In the cross-functional meeting yesterday, you **said my idea was stupid** (event). When I heard your comments, **I felt embarrassed** (feelings). In the next meeting if you are upset about my ideas, please **describe your concerns specifically without evaluative labels** (specific desired behavior). If you are able to meet my request on this issue, I will feel **more willing to work with you** (positive business need). If you are unable to consider my request, I will have to **aggressively defend my projects** (negative business need).

Like many of you, I have had bosses in the past who have said, "If you don't hear from me, you're doing a good job." Their comments weren't mean-spirited. It was their way of delegating. However, I needed to understand how they felt about my work since I was inventing new roles never before performed in these organizations. The first time this situation happened, I made a plan. After three months, I asked my boss if he would give me a few minutes to talk about my performance. We sat down in his office, and I laid out two sheets of paper. On one sheet were the initial objectives for the job upon which he and I had agreed when I first joined the company. On the second sheet were the activities that I had accomplished in the last three months. I reviewed both sheets with my boss and asked for his thoughts. He said, "Glenn, I like what I hear about your sessions. Joe from distribution said he had good reviews from his staff. Basically, I think you're on track." This feedback felt pretty good, as you can imagine. The second time I approached the lack of feedback with a similar layout. Once I had reviewed my objectives and activities, I asked for feedback. This time the results were not as pleasing. My boss had some serious concerns. He wanted me to redistribute the time spent on my objectives. Did I need to know both types of feedback? I sure did. The point of this story is that we don't have to be passive about feedback, even if the feedback we need is from a boss. However, we need to be prepared to receive valid feedback regardless of the valence of the feedback.

Summary

Chapter 7 identified the conflict-related responsibilities of the facilitative leader. Perceptions of organizational members regarding conflict were discussed. The counterproductive group phenomenon called groupthink was described, and its impact on conflict management was explained. A modified conflict management model based on the best-selling book by Fisher and Ury was illustrated. Use of the Thomas-Kilmann Conflict Styles Inventory to enable teams to identify various favored conflict approaches and to deal with day-to-day issues was explained. Finally, a feedback process, called E-FAB, was shown to be effective in aiding employees to create a positive feedback environment.

Questions from Chapter 7

1. If you could eliminate all conflict in your life, would you?
   A. Why?
   B. Why not?
2. Describe the last three conflict situations in which you found yourself. What were the reasons for and outcomes of this conflict?
3. Have both you and another person or group ever realized positive outcomes from a conflict? How so?
4. If you have a poor relationship with a person in one of the conflicts identified above, how can you change your communication to improve the relationship to such a level that the conflict can be addressed effectively?
5. What conflict style do you favor?
   A. Competing? (Winning is very important to you.)
   B. Collaborating? (You like to seek and incorporate the opinions of others.)

    C. Compromising? (You quickly move toward the other person's position to get resolution.)

    D. Avoiding or Deliberate? (You like to gather data and think the situation through.)

    E. Accommodating? (The impact of the conflict solution on your future relationship with the other person is very important.)

6. How does feedback or lack of it impact conflict?

    A. Positively?

    B. Negatively?

Actions from Chapter 7

1. Use the seven-step model based upon Fisher and Ury's work and analyze one of the three conflicts identified above.

2. Write a signposting script in which you indicate to a person involved in one of the conflicts above the communication changes you intend to make to demonstrate more respect for him or her.

3. Identify a criteria for measurement of alternatives that could be generated for one of the conflicts identified above.

4. For one of the conflicts identified above, write a BATNA, things you can do unilaterally if the conflict cannot be resolved.

5. For one of the conflicts identified above, write an E-FAB script to the other person. Remember to use behavioral terms and be respectful.

Small Group Facilitator

The facilitative leader demonstrates all of the behaviors described previously in this book plus distinct small group facilitative behaviors. In this chapter I describe the different roles of the facilitator and techniques for involving team members, dealing with resistance, and intervening to help a team accomplish its role. The different types of facilitation are also covered in this chapter. Facilitation has a dual focus of enabling the group process and accomplishing the product or task. The facilitator is concerned primarily with the process of how a team interacts. Most of the techniques described in this chapter focus on enabling the group process. However, the facilitator is also concerned with the product. If the facilitator is not able to assist the team in creating a product, his or her services will not be valued in the future.

Things Facilitators Do

Let me describe eight things that facilitators do to carry out their roles. First, they encourage and clarify the team's communication. All of the behaviors of the facilitator reflect a respect for the input and ideas of each team member. Encouragement demonstrates a respect for the potential of a team member's thoughts and clarification questions highlight the value of a comment. The second role of the facilitator is to test for agreement. The test for agreement is performed at various times throughout a team meeting. There are low to high levels of tests of agreement. A low-level test of agreement is a simple question, followed by a pause. An example is, "Do we all feel another meeting is necessary, as Terry suggested?" A higher-level test of agreement is a question followed by a pause and then brief eye contact with each participant. An even higher-level test of agreement adds an individual question to each participant. An example is, "What do you think, Joe? How do you feel, Jane? Any thoughts, Jay?" An effective facilitator uses a number of agreement tests in each session.

The third facilitator role is to protect team members. If team members feel that they are attacked or hurt by other team members, they lose faith in you as the facilitator. As part of a program for a power company on conflict management, I was facilitating a discussion one day about the types of conflicts they had experienced in their organization. I asked for an illustration from the group. Phil said, "Yeah, I have a story. Let me use Walt as an example." I looked over at Walt and noticed that he stiffened up. I asked Walt how he felt about being used as an example. He exclaimed, "Well, I don't like it." I turned back to Phil and commented, "Walt is not comfortable with being used as an example. Use some other example." Phil thought for a moment and replied, "No, I'll just use Walt." The two participants were sitting across from one another in an open U-shaped room configuration. I stepped between them, holding my hands out like a traffic cop. I strongly suggested that I was not comfortable with Walt being used since he wasn't comfortable with it. Another team member interjected with a separate illustration that was descriptive. Several times I have actually called a break to protect a participant. Be aware that as a facilitator, one cannot guarantee to protect each individual every time. However, team member protection is an obligation of the facilitator.

The fourth facilitative role is to maintain confidentiality about the group's proceedings. Team members must have confidence that the facilitator will not take confidential statements made in a session and share them outside of the session in ways that are intended to hurt an individual.

Actively listening throughout the session is the fifth facilitative role. Listening is probably the single most important behavior of the small group facilitator. I described in Chapter 3 the verbal and non-verbal behaviors that result in effective listening. An individual's credibility as a facilitator is fundamentally linked to his or her ability to demonstrate listening skills. While listening to team members, it is important to accept information even if it is incomplete. We all communicate differently, at different speeds, and with different organization patterns. Sometimes an incomplete thought thrown out to the team can be the catalyst for the most productive solution. Put the incomplete thought on the flip chart and let it simmer. Usually others will assist by adding to the incomplete thought. Paying attention to all ideas, either complete or incomplete, is part of a competent facilitator's listening skills.

The sixth role of the facilitator is to set a positive tone in a meeting. The facilitator should not be superficially positive about the issues being discussed and should not arbitrarily dismiss the concerns of team members. After fully listening, the facilitator should ask questions about the team's next proactive step. The facilitator also focuses on what can be done rather than on what can't be done.

Modeling effective behaviors in the meeting and on the job is the seventh facilitative role. I suggest that as we learn these behaviors and roles, we need to demonstrate them in all aspects of our lives. If we are highly facilitative in a meeting, yet ignore the same people outside the session, we will be labeled fakes. Learn and practice your new behaviors in all aspects of your life. Be as consistent as you can both in and out of team meetings.

The final, but far from least important, role is that of building consensus. All the roles and behaviors described in this chapter are designed to enable team consensus. Think about the word consensus for a minute. Write down your definition. Some describe consensus as a majority rule process. Others describe consensus as 100 percent agreement that a particular path of action is the best action. The word consensus as used by facilitators today means a team's total commitment to support a particular course of action. The chosen course of action may not be the first choice of some or most of the participants. However, all team members, given the nature of the issue being addressed, believe that the chosen course of action will best serve the team's needs as a whole. Another way of putting it is that the chosen course of action is the best, doable solution. Consensus building takes time. It is not the quickest process. Team members must have agreement to actively participate in discussions with open minds. The communication skills of team members must be well developed. In addition to good communication skills, team members must have respectful relationships. Team members must not only be willing to come to agreement, they must have a determination to come to agreement. I have worked with teams that began a discussion with the opposite intention, that of thwarting any agreement. Also, consensus is most possible when all team members focus on superordinate goals. Superordinate goals are the largest and most important goals of the organization that impact everyone in the company. The true test of consensus is whether or not team members put their energies into supporting the decision and making it a reality.

Involvement Techniques

Adults can be excited and involved or bored and withdrawn. Team members have many life experiences that enhance their contribution to problem solving. It is important to involve them in as many ways as possible. Here are six techniques that have been proven successful in enabling team member involvement in problem solving or planning meetings.

First, break the team into subgroups to discuss the issue at hand. Ask the subgroup to appoint a spokesperson to report key learnings or main points to the entire group. At times, it is useful to assign both groups the same topic to check the level of agreement in the team. At other times you can cover more items by assigning different topics to each subgroup. Have each breakout group record their points on a flip chart so they can share them more easily with the whole group.

Second, use questioning techniques at the beginning, middle, and end of the session. A great deal of the time the facilitator should be thinking about questions that will assist the team in furthering productive discussion and problem solving. Third, use the round robin or other brainstorming techniques described in Chapter 5. Fourth, show the group that you value their expertise on the issue at hand. Make positive statements about team members' comments. Make statements that help the team members understand that you know you don't have all of the answers. Fifth, sit down when a participant is speaking. This technique is useful when a quiet person makes a comment or when you want to get down to the level of the participants for equalization.

Sixth, use proxemics. Move toward or away from individual team members. Movement should be equalized around the room. Don't root yourself in one spot or behind a podium. However, be aware of nervous movement that could have distracting effects. Sometimes a facilitator will take a step toward a participant to designate his or her turn to speak, then step back to give the participant the floor. If the participant appears to be repeating his or her point or speaks too long, the facilitator can take a couple steps toward him or her which is a nonverbal signal to wrap up the thought being presented.

Dealing with Resistance

In some area of our lives, we have all been resistant to some proposal or action. Since resistance is not foreign to us, we should keep in mind that the resistant team member has some reason or reasons for being resistant. It is important not to take resistant behaviors personally. Focus on the content of the resistance and on problem solving with the resistant team members and the rest of the team. A number of different resistant behaviors are common among team members. The facilitator has two major methods for dealing with disruptive individuals during the course of the meeting. One of these methods is to work with the resistant person head-on, that is, to confront him or her and otherwise attempt to contract for more appropriate behavior. The second method is to allow the other team members present to work with the resister. The important consideration is that the facilitator has to be aware of how the chosen intervention will impact the task completion. The facilitator must be careful to remember the other team members because they can be made anxious by these techniques. The facilitator can inadvertently put the resistant team member in an underdog position, thereby gaining sympathy for the resistor from other meeting participants. There is a good chance that others in the meeting are just as annoyed as the facilitator is about the disruptive behavior, and there are ways to use that situation to maintain control. Facilitators can use the other team members to mediate disruptive behavior by encouraging others to express their feelings about the resistant behavior. Sometimes, however, these strategies do not succeed completely, and the facilitator needs different techniques.

Let me describe eight techniques for dealing with resistant team members. These techniques are meant to maintain the facilitator's ability to conduct a productive interchange among members. First, try to get the resistant team member to agree to cooperate for this one meeting. Ask the resistant person to agree not to argue from a familiar, fixed position. Two, work out your differences before the meeting, possibly with a third-party facilitator. Three, structure the meeting to include frequent discussion of the process of the meeting itself. Fourth, have the team members establish ground rules to avoid polarization. For example, have people couch their discussion in terms of needs rather than right or wrong dichotomies. Fifth, post all points raised on a given topic, without names. This makes the information available to all participants and can lessen repetition. Sixth, reflect the feelings of the resistor. "By the way you are speaking, I can tell you really care about this issue."

Seventh, use the parking lot technique to post concerns that are not pertinent to the discussion at hand. The parking lot is simply a flip chart sheet with the words "Parking Lot" written on it that is taped on the wall. Other common names for the parking lot technique are dangling ends or unfinished issues. What you call it is not really important. If irrelevant items come up, ask permission to park them in the parking lot for the time being. The most important part of the parking lot technique is that you address the issue with the team member who identified the item at the end of the meeting. Finally, seek areas of agreement and begin your responses by defining that agreement.

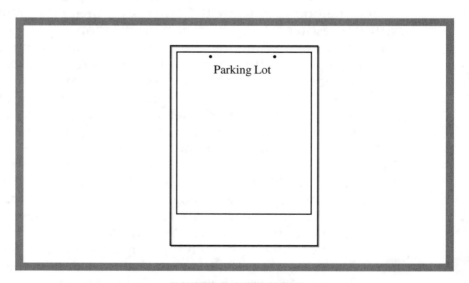

FIGURE 8-1. PARKING LOT

Seldom do I hear a team member's comment that I can't find something with which to agree. You can also agree with the individual's need to be heard and supported. People who resist in meetings have energy that can sometimes be channeled productively. The best outcome and the desired one is that the person who is often disruptive becomes an effective meeting participant.

There are other techniques called interventions that are at times useful for enabling a team. An intervention is anything a facilitator does that modifies the group's behavior toward the group's stated or desired goals. Some common interventions are boomerang, refocus on the agenda, refer to ground rules, highlight and clarify words, reframe the problem, use "I" statements, ask What or How questions, or use a pause. The boomerang technique involves throwing the question back to the questioner. Many times a team member asks a question as a means of getting the floor to state his or her thoughts. As with all of these interventions, a facilitative leader must demonstrate more than just one favored technique. One trainee of mine fixated upon the boomerang technique. I observed him using it three times in a row in response to questions of a team member. Finally, a team member responded, "Dammit, I asked you." The facilitator needs to know when to state an opinion in order to be genuine.

Refocusing on the agenda is an intervention that consists of asking a question as to the relevance of a comment to the agenda item being discussed. "Joe, I understand that our staffing is not up to budget. How does that relate to our agenda item of transportation safety?" Joe will then explain the connection or acknowledge the lack of it. Either outcome furthers the team toward its goal. Highlighting and clarifying words means to capture a particular thought and ask for more information or clarification. "Sally, you mentioned what sounds like an acronym, MAR. Could you explain what that means?" Referring to the ground rules can be an effective intervention. "Joe, one of our ground rules is to give everyone a chance to speak, and I noticed that you have talked most of the ten minutes since the last break. Are you still willing to work within this ground rule?" Reframing the problem is a useful intervention when a team's creativity is waning. "So, folks, how would we address this problem if all our employees were housed in one building?" "I" statements are used as an intervention to say things that the group may be feeling but are uncomfortable saying. "Sally, I'm uncomfortable when you criticize people who are not in the meeting." Asking How or What questions moves the group from blaming to problem solving. Pauses are also effective interventions. They allow the group to think about the comments made and to choose a path forward. Pauses also highlight disruptive behaviors and could enable changed behavior.

Types of Facilitators

The concept of facilitation can be demonstrated in a number of organizational roles. This chapter focuses on the behaviors of the neutral small group facilitator. Sometimes called a stand-up facilitator, this individual is usually not a member of the team being facilitated. He or she has no vested interest in the outcome of the team's decision making. Therefore, the neutral facilitator is focused primarily on the team's process. He or she is not oblivious to the task accomplishment, though. If the neutral facilitator focuses on the process with little attention to the task, the task may not get completed. When that failure occurs, the facilitator is not asked to help the team in the future. Therefore, facilitators who do not help teams succeed with their tasks are weeded out by lack of requests for their services.

The member facilitator is any team member who is sitting at the problem-solving table and demonstrates the behaviors described in this chapter. Most of the facilitator's behaviors make sense for a number of employees. A team member can use facilitative techniques, suggest involvement techniques, or assist in dealing with resistant team members. When more and more team members demonstrate these types of facilitative behaviors, we realize a true organization development process. Some organizations have committed to taking all employees through a facilitator training program both to enable effective team member skills and so that team members better understand what is expected of them in team meetings. If an employee becomes an effective member facilitator, his or her new skills could be invaluable for communicating events outside of the team meeting. Member facilitators have a dual responsibility for the team process and the team task. When one is sacrificed for the other, poor team product is the result.

The final type of facilitator is the facilitative leader. This person is usually the legitimate leader such as a supervisor or manager; however, facilitative leaders can emerge from the group itself. This type of facilitator is, of course, the one to whom this entire book is dedicated. Like member facilitators, team leaders can demonstrate the facilitative techniques described in this chapter in all aspects of their work. Of course, the leader is not neutral. He or she will be held accountable for the accomplishment of the task. The difference between the facilitative leader and traditional leaders is that the facilitative leader is aware of the impact of team process on team task quality and team members' commitment to the team decision. The facilitative leader is competent in most of the behaviors described in this book. He or she assists team members in coping with change; communicates respectfully with team members; focuses on developing team members' learning and helping others to learn from team members' interactions and decisions; understands problem-solving techniques and uses them effectively; and deals positively with conflict when it occurs in a team setting. Leaders who use facilitative behaviors daily may be the most important contributors to the bottom-line success of the organization. All three types of facilitation are important and desirable for any organization.

Given the information in this chapter, do you think that facilitation is more of an art or a science? Some people answer that it is a little of both, which is probably the right answer. There is some science involved in the techniques for dealing with a group of people and administering problem-solving techniques. The most critical components of being a successful facilitator are practice and receiving feedback from others, the art portion of facilitation.

Summary

This chapter was dedicated to the process that the facilitative leader utilizes to enable teams to solve problems and work together effectively. Behaviors that illustrate a good small group facilitator were described. Techniques for involving team members and dealing with resistant team members were explained. Interventions that enable team members to accomplish their goals were identified. Finally, the three different roles of the small group facilitator, the member facilitator, and the facilitative leader were contrasted.

Questions from Chapter 8

1. Why are frequent tests for agreement important for team consensus?
2. How does the parking lot technique enable team focus?
3. What is the effect of facilitative interventions on team products?

4. How do the roles of neutral, member, and facilitative leader differ?

5. How does a facilitator use pauses?

Actions from Chapter 8

1. In your next meeting make a list of the questions you hear. Evaluate the effectiveness of these questions. Rewrite the questions to make them more effective.

2. Describe the resistance you have most recently experienced. Identify how you could use facilitative techniques to address that resistance.

3. In your next team meeting, select involvement techniques that will open the team's communication and practice them.

4. Observe facilitators with whom you come in contact. Record the facilitative techniques you notice. Choose two of these techniques and practice them.

9

Conclusion

We have explored the behaviors of the facilitative leader. This approach to leadership resulted from a culmination of leadership theories from the Great Man theory to McGregor's Theory X and Theory Y. The direction of these leadership styles has been toward more focus on the employee as having the most potential for productivity improvements. In recent years, a series of packages on how to implement this new leadership style have appeared. These leadership processes have ranged from participative management to quality of work life, quality circles, employee involvement, self-directed work teams, and total quality management, among others. Too many times consultants try diligently to differentiate among these approaches. However, when you examine the processes, there is an evolutionary theme that emerges and each new process builds upon the successes of the previous processes. Let's not throw the baby out with the bath water or reinvent the wheel. Let's learn from initiatives that have worked well and improve upon them.

Facilitative leaders are not clones. They demonstrate a variety of unique behaviors. The purpose of this book is to link these behaviors with the five modes of the facilitative leader: enabler of change, respectful communicator, developer of people and teams, master of problem-solving tools, and manager of conflict.

The enabler of change aspect of the facilitative leader represents one of the most critical sets of behaviors today's leaders can demonstrate. Remember, you can't push a pig into a truck. On the other hand, people choose to change every day. With the proper information and education, people can and will move in a common direction. People don't all respond to change in the same way. As a matter of fact, we don't all respond to change circumstances with the same perceptions. Some people love change, support change efforts, and even seek change of the status quo. I call these people the change champions. Others are on the opposite end of this spectrum. They fight change with every ounce of their being. Change is automatically bad to these people. I call this group the "Hell, no, we won't go" group. The third group of people are the fence sitters. They are watching both groups and making decisions accordingly. The enabler of change makes risk taking survivable. Without employees taking risks, stagnation will surely set in. Learning is directly related to risk taking and experimentation.

Another component of enabling change is that of visioning. Vision is a leadership function and a requirement for leadership (Gardner, 1990). Vision is a moving target that develops from an awareness of the contemporary environmental factors and needs and abilities of organizational constituents. Once the vision is developed, then the process of creating consensus of action begins. The change model described in this book involves six steps. These steps are: review the present set of behaviors, define the desired future set of behaviors, communicate the reasons or whys for the change, provide opportunities to learn the new behaviors, give feedback on progress in achieving the new behaviors, and set up rewards for accomplishing the new behaviors. If the facilitative leader addresses all of these steps, most organizational members will choose to change in the direction of the vision. If these steps are thoroughly covered and people don't choose to change, maybe the vision isn't the right one for the organization.

The second mode of the facilitative leader is the respectful communicator. This may be the single most important mode of all. It combines all of the things we say and the nonverbal things we do. The mode is demonstrated when the other person feels like a partner in the business. We develop communication skills throughout our lives with all of our experiences. Every person develops a different field of experience. Nonverbal communication is by far the biggest set of variables to which we pay attention when interpreting messages from others. Listening is a combination of verbal and nonverbal behaviors and is at the core of respectful communicating.

The facilitative leader is a dedicated developer of people. He or she realizes that developing people benefits the business. The facilitative leader first focuses on learning for himself or herself. He or she understands that adults learn through active participation, with appropriate climate, when problems are being solved, at different rates, and with adequate feedback. Facilitative leaders invent mechanisms for creating learning environments for themselves and other organizational members. Feedback techniques, expectations communication, and periodically reviewing key learnings are some of the mechanisms they use.

People development involves both individuals and teams. Individual development can be accomplished by effective performance appraisal and goal setting around organizational objectives. Team development takes time. Teams go through predictable stages. I call these stages introducing, questioning, structuring, inventing, and implementing. Teams need time to talk through and solve their issues. This critical time is called face time. Topics that are useful for face time discussions are how the team will communicate with each other, develop as a team, deal with conflict, interact in meetings, solve problems, and set goals. Finally, the team must honestly discuss their expectations of one another.

As a problem solver, the facilitative leader is action oriented rather than blame placing. He or she focuses on using problem-solving tools in all four phases of the problem-solving process. First, in the problem definition stage, open brainstorming, round robin brainstorming, the affinity process, Delphi technique, and process mapping are all useful to clarify the issue at hand. Prioritization tools that follow the problem definition stage are multivoting, payoff matrix, and Nominal Group Technique. The prioritization tools are used at several phases of the problem-solving process. The second stage is problem analysis. Some tools used to analyze the problem are force field analysis, cause and effect, and five Whys. To accomplish the solution identification stage, stage number three, some of the same tools used in the definition stage are useful. During the solution implementation stage, PERT, Gantt, and flow charts are helpful.

Finally, a stakeholder commitment chart can assist in evaluating any road blocks that may arise among other organizational members. Facilitative leaders also practice effective meeting management techniques. Use of meeting agendas, meeting evaluations, and meeting minutes can continually improve the facilitative leader's ability to use problem-solving tools.

Managing conflict is the final mode of the facilitative leader. It is important to remember that each of us responds to conflict differently and deals with it differently. Five approaches to conflict management are competing, collaborating, compromising, accommodating, and avoiding. Each of these styles creates positive and negative outcomes to the conflict situation. The model described in Chapter 7 has three pieces: the conflict environment, the problem analysis and solving, and the followup. When initially considering the conflict, the relationship and the communication that define it must be analyzed. If the relationship is poor, it is possible to change one's communication to improve the relationship. During the problem-solving segment of the conflict management model, identify criteria that would describe a successful solution. Then, focus on needs and interests rather than positions. Once the needs and interests of the parties involved are identified, options can be brainstormed. Finally, commitment must be clarified. If agreement cannot be accomplished, then each person's BATNA (Best Alternative To a Negotiated Agreement) must be expressed. The BATNA involves the things that people can do if there is no agreement.

Small group facilitation is a forum for all of the above facilitative behaviors. The facilitator assumes a number of effective group responsibilities such as encouraging and clarifying communication, testing for agreement, protecting team members, maintaining confidentiality, actively listening, setting a positive tone, modeling facilitative behaviors, and building consensus. Involvement techniques that the facilitative leader uses are breaking into subgroups, questioning throughout the session, round robin or other brainstorming techniques, showing team members that you value their expertise, sitting down, or proxemics.

Resistance is natural in team interactions. When the facilitative leader encounters resistance, he or she employs some of the following techniques: Try to get cooperation prior to the meeting; use a third-party facilitator to work out differences; discuss process during the meeting; establish ground rules; post points as they arise; reflect the feelings of the resister; use the parking lot technique; and agree with the resister as much as possible. Eight verbal interventions that a facilitator can use that will enable a team to accomplish its objectives are: the boomerang, refocus on the agenda, refer to ground rules, highlight and clarify words, reframe the problem, use "I" statements, ask What or How questions, and use a pause.

All of these small group techniques can be utilized by a neutral person outside the team, by a team member at the table, or by the formal leader of the team. When these behaviors are adopted across the organization, effective interactions can be enhanced.

The role of the facilitative leader is not an easy one. It takes a dual concentration on the task for which the team is held accountable and the process with which team members interact. It takes time to think about the team's future expectations. It takes time to regularly communicate with team members. Peters and Waterman's (1984) concept of Management by Walking Around (MBWA) is useful for the facilitative leader. He or she must model all of the interpersonal and problem-solving skills that team members are expected to demonstrate. Be a continual learner. Keep a list of learnings that you realize daily. Share these learnings with your boss, peers, and subordinates.

Many organizations are choosing behavior change in the direction of the facilitative leader. One such organization is Carr Concrete, a small company producing precast concrete products including burial vaults. Late in 1996, the two brothers who own the company realized that their lassiez-faire leadership role with operations department management had created dissatisfaction among the workers. After several conflicts with the plant manager, the workforce threatened to walk off the job. The owners called me to do a culture check, described in Chapter 4. I interviewed employees from all levels of the organization. The determination was that the environment was focused on production, with little respect for the workers. The owners went right to work to remedy the situation. They transferred the plant manager to a nonsupervisory role. Then they began a collaborative process with all employees to describe the desired culture of Carr Concrete for the future. Excerpts from the Cultural Descriptors that resulted follow:

> *Carr Concrete will provide an environment that encourages integrity, honesty, and high ethical standards of behavior in our dealing with one another and with our customers, suppliers, and neighbors.*
>
> *Carr Concrete expects all employees to respect the rights, personal property, opinions, and judgements of others. . . . It is important that*

everyone in the organization makes his or her best effort to learn how to respect others. It is equally important that the organization assist in this effort by providing guidelines and education.

The management and supervision of Carr Concrete are responsible for maintaining a workplace that encourages and solicits straightforward and open communication, while all employees have the responsibility to ask questions and submit suggestions and ideas. Our corporate culture should be one that encourages questions, facilitates listening to one another, asks opinions, solves problems with teamwork, and recognizes and solves conflicts as quickly as possible. Employees should know what is expected of them and then get regular feedback on their performance from supervisors and management. Communication between employees should be courteous and free of profanity or demeaning or abusive language.

Realizing that no two employees will have exactly the same skills or skill levels, our goal must be to make everyone in our organization as good as they can be. Every employee is valuable to the company and therefore is valuable to all other employees. Each employee has two responsibilities in this area: to do his or her job to the best of his or her ability, and to assist all other employees to do their jobs to the best of their ability. . . . Everyone in the organization needs to be a teacher as well as a student.

. . . The responsibility of management is to encourage, promote, and support this culture with education, training, time, monetary resources, and conviction. If each employee of Carr Concrete will make an effort to proceed toward this goal, we are guaranteed a better place to work.

The above statement is a vision of a work environment designed by a facilitative leader and in which a facilitative leader would flourish. Following the joint development of this statement, plans were made to create new learning opportunities for all employees. The plant manager who was moved became a valued contributor as the company purchasing agent. A new facilitative leader was hired as plant manager, and employees expressed improved morale as the company doubled in size and profits.

The facilitative leader does not interact with every team in exactly the same way. He or she treats team members as individuals. Team members are respected and valued for their contributions. Both positive and constructive feedback are delivered in a timely fashion. Schedule regular feedback time on your calendar every week for different employees. As a manager makes movement toward the facilitative leader role, team members will notice and, in most cases, will encourage the new behaviors. But remember, incremental, persistent personal development plans create more significant behavior change over time.

References

Axtell, R. E. (1993). *Do's and taboos around the world* (3rd ed.). New York: John Wiley and Sons, Inc.

Baird, L. S., Post, J., and Mahon E. (1990). *Management: Functions and responsibilities.* New York: Harper & Row.

Barker, J. A. (1992). *Future edge: Discovering the new paradigms of success.* New York: William Morrow and Company.

Bass, M. B. (1990). *Bass and Stogdill's handbook of leadership: Theory, research, and managerial applications* (3rd ed.). New York: The Free Press.

Bellah, R. N., Madsen, R., Sullivan, W. M., Swidler, A., and Tipton, S.M. (1985) *Habits of the heart: Individualism and commitment in American life.* New York: Harper & Row.

Block, P. (1981). *Flawless consulting: A guide to getting your experience used.* San Diego, CA: University Associates.

Dalkey, N. (1969). *The Delphi method: An experimental study of group opinion.* Santa Monica, CA: Rand Corporation.

Depree, M. (1992). *Leadership jazz.* New York: Doubleday.

Evans, J. R., and Lindsay, W. M. (1996). *The management and control of quality* (3rd ed.). Minneapolis, MN: West Publishing.

Fernandez, J. P. (1993). *The diversity advantage: How American business can outperform Japanese and European companies in the global marketplace.* New York: Lexington Books.

Fisher, R., and Ury, W. (1991). *Getting to yes: Negotiating agreement without giving in.* New York: Penguin Books.

Funk & Wagnall's New Encyclopedia. (1996). New York: Lippincott and Crowell, Publishers.

Gardner, J. W. (1990). *On leadership.* New York: The Free Press.

Hammer, M., and Champy, J. (1993). *Reengineering the corporation: A manifesto for business revolution.* New York: HarperCollins Publisher.

Harrison, R. (1970). Nonverbal communication: Explorations into time, space, action, and object. In J. Campbell & H. Helper (eds.), *Dimensions in communication.* Belmont, CA: Wadsworth.

Hersey, P., and Blanchard, K. (1982). *Management of organizational behavior: Utilizing human resources* (4th ed.). Englewood Cliffs, NJ: Prentice Hall.

Janis, I. L. (1972). *Victims of groupthink.* Boston: Houghton Mifflin.

Kayser, T. A. (1990). *Mining group gold: How to cash in on the collaborative brain power of a group.* El Segundo, CA: Serif Publishing.

Knowles, M. S. (1980). *The modern practice of adult education: From pedagogy to andragogy.* Chicago: Association Press.

Lewin, K., Lippitt, R., and White, R. K. (1939). Patterns of aggressive behavior in experimentally created social climates. *Journal of Social Psychology, 10,* 271–301.

Likert, R. (1967). *Human organization.* New York: McGraw-Hill.

Looram, J. (1985). The transition meeting: Taking over a new management team. *Supervisory Management, 29–36.*

Maurer, R. (1996). *Beyond the wall of resistance: Unconventional strategies that build support for change.* Austin, TX: BardBooks, Inc.

Mayo, E. (1947). *The human problems of an industrial civilization.* Boston: Harvard Business School.

McCroskey, J., and Wheeless, L. (1976). *Introduction to human communication.* New York: Allyn and Bacon.

McGregor, D. (1960). *The human side of enterprise.* New York: McGraw-Hill.

Mohrman, S. A., Cohen, S. G., and Mohrman, A. M. (1995). *Designing team-based organizations: New form of knowledge work.* San Francisco: Jossey Bass Publishers.

Peters, T. J., and Waterman, R. H. (1984). *In search of excellence: Lessons from America's best run companies.* New York: Warner Communications.

Ray, J. H., and Ray, R. G. (1995). Social relations and leisure activities in underground coal mines of Northern Appalachia. *Tennessee Anthropologist, 20*(1), 18–34.

Ray, R. G. (1988). The relationship of participation and communication satisfaction to productivity as mediated by locus of control. (Doctoral dissertation, Ohio University, Athens, Ohio). *Dissertation abstracts international, 49*, 2022A.

Ray, R. G. (1993). Portal to portal: My experience mining coal in Ohio. *Appalachian Journal: A Regional Studies Review, 21*(1), 24–49.

Ray, R. G. (1995). A training model for implementing self-directed work teams. *Organization Development Journal, 13*(1), 51–62.

Ray, R. G. (1997). Developing internal consultants. *Training and Development. 51*(7), 30–34.

Ray, R. G., and Brown, C. J. (1997). Using TQM to lead culture change in J. J. Phillips & E. F. Holton (eds.), *In action: Leading organizational change* (pp. 247–260). Alexandria, VA: American Society for Training and Development.

Ray, R. G., Hines, J., and Wilcox, D. (1994). Training internal facilitators. *Training and Development, 48*(11), 45–48.

Ray, R. G., and Stapleton, K. (1998). The role of facilitation in team breakthroughs. In J.J. Phillips, S. D. Jones & M. M. Beyerlein (eds.), *In action: Developing high-performance work teams (pp. 91-112).* Alexandria, VA: American Society for Training and Development.

Ray, R. G., Warner, A., Potash, S., and Ford, V. (1997). Using a cross-functional team to design a performance appraisal instrument. Manuscript submitted for publication.

Richardson, F. D. and Ray, R. G. (In press). *Thinking strategically in a changing healthcare environment.* In J. Rabin (ed.), *Handbook of strategic management.* New York: Marcel Dekker Publisher.

Roethlisberger, F. L., and Dickson, W. (1939). *Management and the worker.* New York: John Wiley & Sons.

Schein, E. H. (1992). *Organizational culture and leadership* (2nd ed.). San Francisco: Jossey-Bass Publishers.

Schramm, W. (1954). *The process and effects of mass communication.* Urbana, IL: University of Illinois Press.

Senge, P. M. (1990). *The fifth discipline: The art and practice of the learning organization.* New York: Doubleday Currency.

Slater, R. (1993). *The new GE: How Jack Welch revived an American institution.* Homeword, IL: Business One Irwin.

Stogdill, R. M., and Shartle, C. L. (1948). Methods for determining patterns of leadership behavior in relation to organization structure and objectives. *Journal of Applied Psychology, 32,* 286–291.

Thomas, K. W., and Kilmann, R. H. (1974). *Thomas-Kilmann conflict mode instrument.* Tuxedo, NY: XICOM.

Tichy, N. M., and Sherman, S. (1993). *Control your destiny or someone else will: Lessons in mastering change—from the principles Jack Welch is using to revolutionize GE.* New York: HarperCollins.

van de Ven, A. H. (1973). *An applied experimental test of alternative decision-making.* Canton, OH: Center for Business and Economic Research Press, Kent State University.

van Fleet, D. D., and Yukl, G. A. (1989). A century of leadership research. In W. E. Rosenbach and R. L. Taylor (eds.), *Contemporary issues in leadership* (2nd ed.). Boulder, CO: Westview Press.

Watzlawick, P., Beavin, J., and Jackson, D. (1967). *Pragmatics of human communication: A study of interactional patterns, pathologies, and paradoxes.* New York: Norton.

Weihrich, H. and Rigny, A. (1980). Toward System 4 through transactional analysis. *Journal of Systems Management, 31*(7), 30–36.

Weisbord, M. R. (1987). *Productive workplaces: Organizing and managing for dignity, meaning, and community.* San Francisco: Jossey-Bass.

Wellins, R. S., Byham, W. C., and Dixon, G. R. (1994). *Inside teams: How 20 world-class organizations are winning through teamwork.* San Francisco: Jossey Bass Publishers.

Wheatley, M. J. (1992). *Leadership and the new science: Learning about organization from an orderly universe.* San Francisco: Berrett-Koehler Publishers.

Index